Flower Arranging

Flower Arranging

Barbara Pearce

Optimum Books

Photographic acknowledgments
All photographs published in this book are the property of the
Hamlyn Group Picture Library with the exception of the
following: Hirmer Verlag, Munich: page 6. Wallace Collection,
London: page 8 right. Trustees of the Wedgwood Museum,
Barlaston, Staffs.: page 8 bottom left. A. F. Kersting, London:
page 10. Pat Brindley, Cheltenham: pages 53, 54 top right, 54
bottom left, 55 right, 56 right, 57 bottom right, 62.

Photographs on pages 116, 117 and 119 were taken at All Saints
Church, Binfield, Berkshire, by kind permission of the Reverend
Owen Blatchly.

This edition published by Optimum Books 1983

Prepared by
Dean's International Publishing
A division of The Hamlyn Publishing Group Limited
London · New York · Sydney · Toronto
Astronaut House, Feltham, Middlesex, England

Some of the material in this book is from *The World of Flower Arranging*
published by The Hamlyn Publishing Group Limited in 1982.

Printed in Spain by Graficromo s.a., Cordoba, Spain

Contents

1 The Development of Flower Arranging

Flower arrangement is by no means a new conception, as can be seen by studying the skills of the temple builder, potter, stonemason, woodcarver and painter, who frequently reproduced in their work many aspects of everyday life. From earliest times man has devised aesthetic satisfaction from using flower shapes and colours to create forms of beauty.

As is known from wall paintings in Egyptian tombs, as far back as 2,500 B.C. sacred lotus flowers were arranged in vases of a very unusual kind, some having extra spouts at the sides to support the heavy-headed flower, and mainly being heavily decorated. The Greeks and Romans had little interest in placing flowers in arrangements, but used them in garlands and wreaths made for personal adornment. With the decline of the Roman Empire in the fifth century A.D. flower art in the West seems to have completely disappeared until its re-emergence in medieval Europe.

Japanese flower arrangement, being a linear art, is very different from Western flower arrangement. It dates from the sixth century when it was introduced to Japan by Buddhist monks from China where formal line arrangement was a temple art. By the sixteenth century huge exhibitions and competitions were held throughout the country but a more informal approach to flower arrangement was rapidly gaining popularity. It was not until the latter half of the nineteenth century though that women were allowed to study the art of flower arrangement. Today many of our more simple arrangements are derived from Japanese arrangements, both the classical and less stylized.

In medieval times the monks in Europe cultivated gardens where they grew herbs and flowers for medicinal purposes, as can be seen in stained glass windows, paintings and murals, but it was not until the Renaissance, with the cultivation of gardens as forms of beauty in their own right, that the growing of flowers was firmly established throughout Europe. Italian books of this period tell not only of the cultivation of flowers, but also the care of cut flowers. Flower arrangement at this time was unimaginative and stiff, but in the seventeenth century flowers were carefully positioned to show curving lines and forms, resulting in lovely graceful arrangements.

In the Low Countries, painters were turning their attention to capturing the beauty of flowers in full, mixed arrangements. These paintings differed a great deal, from the fulsome bouquets of garden flowers, such as those of Jan Breughel, to the magnificently coloured profusions of fruits and flowers as portrayed by Jan van Huysum. All the paintings of that period delight the eye with their exquisite details of blossoms and foliage and beautiful forms.

The flower arrangements favoured by the French in the seventeenth century were quite similar. Among the most outstanding of the French artists was the painter and engraver Jean Baptiste Monnoyer, who had originally painted in the Flemish tradition. His arrangements of

The ancient Egyptian love of flowers and formalized arrangement of them is well illustrated by the wall paintings in their tombs. In this scene, painted on the plaster of Menna's tomb at Thebes, a stylized clump of papyrus provides an interesting centrepiece while the surface of the water beneath is patterned with sacred lotus flowers.

Left: Buddhist monks from China introduced flower arranging into Japan in the sixth century. This group is typical of the early central flower arrangements which were used as offerings before shrines and tombs.

Above: This porcelain vase from Arita in Japan dates from about 1680. The delicate flower arrangements inlaid in enamel reflect the growing popularity of the art in Japan where huge exhibitions and competitions were being held from the sixteenth century onwards.

Left: The ancient Romans used flowers and foliage for personal adornment rather than interior decoration. Garlands and wreaths are frequently depicted in their art, as in this detail from a Pompeiian mural painting of Iphigenia in Aulis.

Above: Outstanding among French flower painters of the seventeenth century was Jean Baptiste Monnoyer. This engraving of a basket of flowers shows that his delicacy of touch did not desert him even with a fairly large arrangement.

Right: This elegant profusion of flowers is typical of work from the hand of Jan van Huysum. Like other eighteenth-century painters from the Low Countries he depicted large arrangements with a variety of different flowers, each one picked out in exquisite detail.

This Quiver Vase was one of many pieces produced by the English firm of Wedgwood in the eighteenth century.

flowers show grace and delicacy even in mass arrangements which are never overwhelming.

Exquisite vases were being made in France in the eighteenth century, one of the most famous makers of ornamental porcelain being Sèvres, while in England Josiah Wedgwood was justly famous for his ceramic vases. The British had long enjoyed a reputation for being flower lovers, gardens having existed as far back as the Middle Ages, when flowers were grown for herbal use and religious festivals, with cut flowers being woven into garlands as in Greek and Roman times. By the sixteenth century English homes were filled with fragrant flowers which served to sweeten the air as well as decorate the rooms. During the summer months greenery and flowers were placed in the fireplaces, a custom which still exists today. In the seventeenth and eighteenth centuries garlands of flowers and arrangements in baskets were depicted in wood carvings such as those by Grinling Gibbons.

There is little recorded about flowers in America in colonial times, though there were many lovely wild flowers and shrubs and also the flowers brought over by settlers for medicinal purposes. Vases are known to have been imported so probably any flower arrangements were informal ones. Today arrangements which are a combination of a mass arrangement and a line arrangement are popular. They allow for a great deal of self-expression, blending as they do the influences of both the West and the East.

In the Victorian era books and magazines were available to give advice on all aspects of flower care, from growing them to treating them before placing in water. House plants were much in vogue as well as exotic and ornamental plants grown in conservatories. The famous épergnes of fruit and flowers and the glass domes containing fresh or dried

Left: The British have a long tradition as lovers of flowers and gardens. As far back as early medieval times flowers were being specially grown for religious festivals and were appearing with great frequency in illuminated manuscripts such as the one illustrated here, painstakingly produced by an English monk in the quiet seclusion of his monastery.

Below: Flowers have long been an accepted part of the domestic scene. Even at the breakfast table, depicted here by the modern French artist Bonnard, the simply arranged vase of flowers does not seem out of place beside the cups and saucers and homely brown teapot.

flowers are known to all today, and sweet-scented nosegays of carefully selected flowers such as sweet peas, lilies of the valley or violets were also extremely fashionable. Flower arrangements were usually very gay and colourful, very full at the beginning of the period but with less flowers in them towards the end, though they normally always included some foliage or greenery.

In the present century Constance Spry played a major part in creating the style of flower arranging now popular in Britain and elsewhere. Well known for her love of flowers, both in the garden and in arrangements, she did much to establish natural arrangements and encourage the use of unusual plant material in them.

The arrangement I have created here depicts a Dutch or Flemish flower painting of the seventeenth century. I did not copy a particular painting but took into account the colours, style and flowers used by the artists. The flowers chosen

Overflowing flower baskets and festoons were among the favourite themes of Grinling Gibbons. His superb craftsmanship is well illustrated in this detail from the Carved Room at Petworth House, West Sussex. Cherubs' heads support a mixed flower arrangement intricately carved in limewood whilst crossed cornucopiae disgorge fountains of wheat, fruit and flowers – all to celebrate the achievements of his patron, the Duke of Somerset. Similar work is quite commonly found in English stately homes of the seventeenth and eighteenth centuries.

are one yellow fritillary, two yellow gladioli, two white and three red border carnations, cherry blossom, malus blossom, one blue hyacinth, one blue iris, one stem of clivia, two purple and two pink and white tulips, two stems *Viburnum opulus* 'Sterile' (guelder rose), two yellow roses, purple hellebores, three pheasant eye narcissi, four red ranunculus and *Viburnum tinus*. These provide a variety of colour and shape.

The container, a black urn with a green tinge, was fitted with wire netting, and being fairly deep it was unnecessary to use a pinholder or florists' foam. The netting is placed in as described in Chapter 7. The picture frame completes the effect of a painting. It has metal pieces attached at the back to enable it to stand. From time to time when establishing the outline, it helps to place the frame in front of the arrangement to ensure the flowers fit into the space inside the frame.

Begin three-quarters back in the container, as is usual for a facing arrangement, with a yellow gladiolus, because it is pointed in shape and the colour shows

up well. On the right of this place a spray of cherry blossom, and position the other gladiolus in front of it. On the opposite side place a small-flowered red ranunculus. The Dutch Group requires a more rounded top than is normal for a facing arrangement. A stem of malus blossom becomes the widest point on the right side with a red border carnation on the other side. The longest flower at the front is a purple hellebore.

With the main outline established, place the fritillary low into the right of the centre with the orange clivia higher on the opposite side to balance it. With the large flowers in place return to the outline, and keeping it fairly round at the back and a semi-circular shape at the front, fill in with flowers between the main outline points. With this group it is unnecessary to be particular with the grouping but the flowers should be well balanced and evenly spread throughout the arrangement. *Viburnum tinus* is used to help fill in and cover the wire netting. Variation of stem length is still necessary with Dutch arrangements and interest is

added to the arrangement if some flowers are turned sideways. All the stems radiate from the centre.

To add weight to the arrangement, place a bird's nest at the base of the urn. The one shown in the photograph contains artificial eggs. Nests were often de-picted in paintings though sometimes an open rose or another kind of flower was used. Instead of a bird's nest a shell could be used, or an artificial butterfly placed on a flower in the arrangement itself. This type of arrangement is suitable for a traditional setting.

An arrangement in an urn inspired by the Dutch flower paintings. Try to include flowers similar to those used by the painters and in the same mixture of colours. The arrangement is described at the end of this chapter.

2 Principles of Flower Arranging

The three tallest flowers in a facing arrangement are positioned in the centre of the container. Each is a different length, the one with the tallest stem and smallest flower being in the centre.

When starting to learn how to arrange flowers in a container, which can be any type of vase, bowl or indeed anything in which flowers can be attractively arranged, it is helpful to follow a few guidelines. These guidelines are not rules, and at times you may have to adapt them; for example certain shaped flowers may prove impossible to obtain or you may not have exactly the right container.

Positioning flowers in an arrangement

In most arrangements you should have an uneven number of large flowers in the centre to give weight and consequently a feeling of holding the arrangement together. These should vary in stem length, the largest of the flowers being placed in lowest. The smaller flowers around the edge and also throughout the arrangement need to be long-stemmed. Begin with the smallest flowers at the top of the arrangement and place the larger of the smaller flowers lower down on the periphery. When the important centre flowers and main outline ones are in position, complete the arrangement with small, long-stemmed flowers, medium-sized flowers and foliage placed so that the flowers are evenly distributed throughout the arrangement. When looking at a completed arrangement from the side you need to see fairly dainty-looking flowers emerging slightly longer.

Positioning the tallest flowers

In a facing arrangement the first flower placed in is usually the tallest, so that the height of the arrangement is established. It is positioned three-quarters of the way back in the container. This is because if the arrangement were to start at the back of the container, the flowers which would be necessary to fill the space and come well out over the front edge would appear to bulge in the centre and the shape would be lost. The tallest flower should be a bud or small flower, so the arrangement is lighter at the top and does not have a top-heavy appearance. A second flower, about half a head to a head shorter, is placed at the side close to the first flower, and a third flower half a head shorter than the second flower is placed close to the tallest flower on the opposite side to the second flower. Each flower should be slightly larger than the one before it.

The tallest flowers in an arrangement to be seen from all sides are placed in the centre of the container, using a bud or small flower, and having slightly larger

In an arrangement which is to be seen from all sides the tallest flowers should be positioned in the centre. The flower with the smallest head is in the middle with three or four other flowers, varying in length but all slightly shorter, around it.

flowers of varying lengths around the tallest one. When using wire netting, a pinholder or florists' foam, it is advisable to place the stems of the centre flowers quite close together which helps to keep them stable. The tallest flowers are not necessarily placed in first in an all-round arrangement or table centre; often the main flowers around the outline edge are put in first to establish the size of the arrangement.

Placing flowers over the edge of the container

An arrangement should ideally blend with its container and sit happily there without looking detached. This is achieved by making sure flowers are placed in close to the rim of the arrangement, using stems where possible which have a natural curve downwards, and placing the stems horizontally over the edge of the container – just far enough to have a good supply of water at all times.

If an arrangement is to be seen from all sides, the horizontally placed flowers need to be all the way round the edge of

the container; when the arrangement is to be seen only from the front, then a lovely semi-circular sweep from both sides to the front is required.

How stems radiate in an arrangement

To have stems radiating from the tallest flower in an arrangement helps the flowers to look as if they are growing naturally, as if they are one plant with flowers and leaves growing from it. This does not mean all the flower stems are touching the tallest flower, but point in its direction from whichever position they are placed into the container.

Placing stems correctly in a container

The stem of the flower needs to be positioned in such a way as to ensure the head of the flower is in the required position. This also applies to leaves. Because the stems radiate in an arrangement, try to avoid crossing them as they could become entangled in the container, causing problems if you wanted to alter a stem's length after completing an arrangement. If you tried to remove it, other flowers might topple and would then have to be replaced, or you might even have to begin the arrangement again. If each flower has its own place to go into the container, with its stem only in a short way and not crossing with the one beside it, providing the water is well up to the rim of the vase at all times, everything should then be satisfactory.

If a flower is not positioned correctly, it is preferable to take it out and put it where it is required rather than to try to pull it to that position, as this will cause stems to cross each other.

Variation of stem lengths

Using various stem lengths throughout an arrangement, around the periphery and in the centre, helps to obtain an attractive and more interesting arrangement. It is better not to have two stems of the same length side by side. Wherever possible, you need to place smaller flowers in fairly high, larger flowers in low to give depth to the arrangement, with the in-between lengths being medium-sized flowers. Arranging in this method enables you to see each flower individually, and so to its best advantage.

How to avoid overcrowding flowers

A less crowded arrangement looks more pleasant than one which is overfull, though obviously you do not want to have any of the mechanics of the arrangement, such as the wire netting or pin-

Place flowers which are to go over the edge of the container horizontally, using ones with curved stems where possible and having them going in and out around the edge to form a broken line.

holder, showing or to see too many bare stems which would give the arrangement an unfinished look. Flowers should be evenly distributed throughout the container and placed for each flower to be seen individually. It should always be remembered that when a flower is used in its bud or half open stage it will before too long open into a larger flower, so counteract this by allowing extra space.

Foliage needs to be used sparingly. Used to hide netting and cover some of the longer-stemmed flowers it can be most attractive, but too much could make your arrangement look a little bit like a forest.

Grouping of flowers

Grouping of flowers, which applies to both mixed coloured and mixed flowered arrangements, is an important factor in obtaining a balanced effect. In a facing arrangement flowers and foliage should be chosen for weight and colour on either side. Having a spiky kind of flower and a single flower head on either side of the arrangement helps with grouping. A main flower and large leaves grouped in the centre brings the arrangement together. The grouping is generally from high on one side of the arrangement to low on the opposite side, with another group going the opposite way. This is achieved with colour as well as with different shaped flowers.

In an all-round arrangement go from one side to the opposite side, merging the colours and flowers slightly so as to make it look less rigid. Grouping in a table centre goes diagonally across the arrangement, but again merge the flowers together slightly.

The facing arrangement in the tazza, shown here, in pink and white enables one to see how the grouping is achieved. In this case the arrangement is symmetrical. In the pottery tazza place a pinholder three-quarters of the way back with netting going over it as shown in Chapter 7. The five different flowers chosen are in two colours so the grouping can be seen more clearly. The pointed flowers of the campanula and the single flowers of the carnations are in white and are one group. The pointed larkspur and the single flowers of the roses are the other group and are in pink. For the centre, there are three peonies, to give weight. The foliage is also grouped through, escallonia with the pink flowers, *Senecio greyii* with the white, and three large hosta leaves for the centre with the peonies. The flowers and foliage are conditioned as described in Chapter 9, and some water is placed into the container.

Stems should radiate from the tallest flower at the back, but the stems around the edge should only be positioned about halfway between the tallest flower and the edge. This helps to prevent the stems crossing each other.

Begin the arrangement by selecting a comparatively small-flowered campanula. This is the tallest flower, at least one and a half times the height of the tazza, and should be secured three-quarters of the way back in the centre of the container. Take a second campanula with a slightly larger flower but a shorter stem and place this a little to the left side of the first campanula so that it is secured through the same hole in the netting and is adjacent to the first stem on the pinholder. Next take a larkspur, cut it a little shorter than the second campanula and place it to the other side (right) of the first campanula, again securing it through the same hole in the netting.

Establish the widest points on each side of the arrangement so that the overall width is roughly the same as the height. Where possible use curved stems for this. Place a campanula on the right and a larkspur on the left, which enables the grouping of the campanula to go from high on the left to low on the right and the larkspur high on the right to low on the left. Both these stems should be three-quarters of the way back in the tazza and of equal length. They should be as horizontal as possible but go into the water. The longest flower over the front edge is a larkspur and it is in a line with the tallest flower at the back.

Next place in the three peonies and three hosta leaves. Place the largest peony low into the centre with a smaller one above this and a little to the right. The third peony goes low over the right front edge. The leaves should be positioned so that one goes over the right front edge, one goes at the back facing the one at the front and the largest leaf goes low into the centre and turned slightly sideways. Next proceed to the outline and, making sure the stems radiate and that they do not exceed the

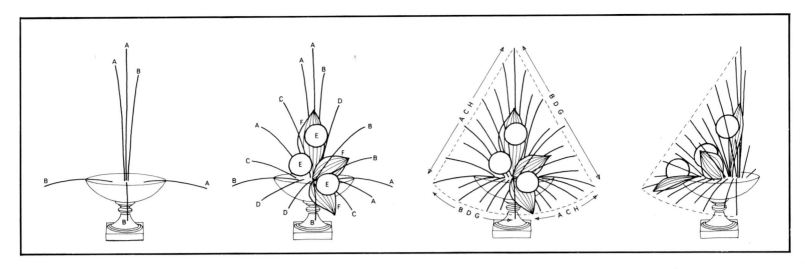

and do not force them into a position that is not natural to their growth. Certain types of flowers grow upright, so it is better not to place them sideways in a container, for example, bulrushes and grasses. Certain leaves also grow upright such as iris and sansevieria, so again keep these straight up in a vase.

It is preferable to have some flowers falling sideways in an arrangement rather than all of them facing the front, especially a flower with an 'eye', that is, a single flower with a flat face. Flowers do face various directions when they are growing, especially if not fully in the sunlight, which gives them a natural curve.

Plant material which naturally hangs over a wall or fence such as *Hedera* (ivy) and *Lonicera* (honeysuckle), looks particularly well placed if put on the edge of the container.

Use of mixed flowers

When using mixed flowers it is an advantage to have at least three different kinds. Two can be used but it does not make such an interesting arrangement. With three kinds you can group one kind each way and have the third type as the main flower in the centre or, as some arrangers prefer to call it, the focal point. If using all one colour with mixed flowers, choose as many different shaped flowers as possible.

How to achieve a broken line around the edge of an arrangement

Having a broken edge makes an arrangement look less set. To prevent it looking as if it has been cut by trimmers, place some flowers a little shorter against one which is slightly longer, and so zig-zag in and out around the periphery. This gives an uneven but natural-looking impression while maintaining the overall triangular shape which gives the arrangement so much of its appeal.

lengths of the main outline flowers which will lose the shape, join up the principal outline flowers around the edge, remembering to keep the flowers in groups. In this case the white flowers extend from high on the left to low on the right with the pink larkspur and roses arranged in the opposite way. Bring the stem lengths down quite sharply at the back and have a good semi-circle around the front. Foliage can be placed in now. Keep the escallonia and rose foliage with the larkspur and roses, and the senecio with the campanula and carnations, and follow the line of the flowers through, placing

some foliage fairly high and some low to cover the netting.

Connect the groups of flowers and foliage through the centre and make sure the flowers are evenly spaced. Check the wire netting is covered, including that at the back of the tazza. Stand away from the arrangement to check the grouping.

Natural flower arrangement

A natural flower arrangement looks more informal and gives the effect that it is growing. Let the branches, leaves and flower stems curve the way they grow

The centre flowers in an arrangement

These are usually the largest flowers, and therefore only a small number are required, such as three, five or seven. It is easier with the placement to have an uneven number rather than an even one, as they go from side to side through the centre. If four were used it would be very easy to place them in a square by mistake, or if maybe six or eight were used it would be easy to place them in twos making the arrangement rather regimented. For a very large arrangement, such as one on a pedestal or plinth, a greater number of flowers would be needed for the centre. An uneven number of leaves can be used instead of flowers for the focal point but again these need to be large, and you can use flowers and leaves together.

Covering wire netting and other mechanics

As has been mentioned earlier, too much 'filler', that is leaves, etc., can spoil the effect of an arrangement, but small pieces of plant material are useful to cover any mechanics which have been used. In an arrangement commencing three-quarters of the way back, a quarter of the container is left free, and covering it with any small pieces of plant material which are available after the arrangement is completed makes it look tidier if seen from the side.

Avoiding too flat an arrangement

Arrangements generally should not look 'flat' when seen from the side. By building out gradually from the tallest flowers at the back to the longer ones over the front edge with lighter weight flowers, you should be able to achieve a triangular effect from this angle, too.

Size of an arrangement in relation to size of the container

The size of the container should be considered carefully when choosing plant material. Generally speaking, if the vase has a stem the proportion of the flowers to the container should be at least one and a half times the height of the container; if the vase is urn shaped then it can be even taller. If it is a shell type vase on a stem then it is better to keep the arrangement low and wide and not too large.

The flowers should be of a size in keeping with the size of the container. Smaller vases need smaller flowers, but a good variety of shapes can still be selected when using mixed flowers. Much bigger containers, such as those which go on to pedestals, need larger and bolder flowers and foliage so that the container does not end up by dominating the arrangement.

Pruning of plant material for an arrangement

Often plant material is too heavy for a particular arrangement, especially when it is to be used near the top. Some of the secondary stems can be carefully cut away and these can be used lower down. Make sure the cuts are not noticeable in the finished arrangement. This can be achieved by cutting at the back of the plant stem so that it cannot be seen from the front, but if this is not possible, then cover it with a flower or leaf when placing the plant material into the arrangement.

Right: An arrangement is best prepared in the actual position it will finally occupy, but a dust sheet needs to be used to protect the floor.

Above: Pruning a spray carnation by carefully cutting away some of the secondary stems to leave a flower of lighter weight.

Where to prepare the arrangement

Ideally this should be where the arrangement is to be situated, because if it is arranged at a different level from where it is to be placed it can look completely wrong when put into position. If this is impossible for various reasons – sometimes one cannot get into a hall early enough to do an arrangement for a reception, or one is not allowed to arrange the flowers on the altar of a church – then measure the height and width of where the arrangement is to be placed and try to find a suitable position of the same height and width on which to arrange them.

When finally placed in their required position they should look correct.

Filling the container with water

It is preferable to only three-quarters fill the container with water before beginning to arrange the flowers and foliage as the water level will rise when the plant material stems are put into position. Fill the container to the rim when the arrangement is complete. Check daily to see if the container needs topping up. It will need more at the beginning than when the flowers have been there a few days.

3 The Choice of Plant Material

The choice of flowers, foliage, fruit, vegetables and moss needs careful consideration when flower arranging in order to keep the correct balance of weight and colour in the arrangement. You may not be able to find some of the flowers and foliage which I have used in the arrangements in this book, but do not let this deter you. There are many other similar plants which can be substituted.

Choice of flowers

For the purposes of arranging, flowers can be classed into three groups. First there are the pointed flowers which have many flowers borne closely on one stem.

The pointed effect is produced because the flowers gradually open in succession starting with the lowest. Those at the top are only in bud form when the flowers at the bottom are at their best and so the spike gradually tapers to a point. Examples include gladioli, larkspur, delphiniums, foxgloves and stocks.

The second group also has many flowers on each stem but each of them is borne on a separate secondary stalk to give a bunchy appearance. Examples include spray chrysanthemums, *Aster novae-belgii* (Michaelmas daisy) and alstroemeria (Peruvian lily). The first two have flowers originating from all down the stem and the alstroemeria has flowers

deriving from one point at the top of the stem.

The third class comprises the flowers which are carried singly at the end of the main stem. These flowers have a variety of shapes. There are both single and double kinds, some with flat faces and some with trumpets. Examples include Papavers (poppies), carnations, daisies and daffodils.

The gladiolus (left) is one of the pointed flowers often used to add lightness to the top of an arrangement. Chrysanthemums (centre) give a bunchy appearance. Flowers on a single stem, such as the daffodil (right), can be single or double.

weight will help to hold the arrangement together and to give solidity. Even when doing a small arrangement you can still use larger leaves in the centre, but these should be in scale with the rest of the plant material. Ideal for this purpose are ivy and scindapsis. An uneven number of leaves are used in the centre. There should not be too many as this would defeat the object of keeping a clean-cut centre. You can also use whole rosettes of leaves in the centre of an arrangement instead of large, single leaves. House plants, aspidistras and caladiums, for example, can be very attractive sources of material.

For our purposes compound leaves can be described as those with many leaves to a stem and these can be grouped with the flowers through an arrangement. It is preferable to have two kinds of this type in a mixed arrangement, so that one kind can be arranged with one group and the other with the second. Examples include pittosporum and senecio, which have quite small individual leaves, and Portuguese laurel and gaultheria which are quite large. When choosing the foliage to go with certain flowers try to get either a

When creating an arrangement of mixed flowers, it is preferable to combine these various shapes remembering when placing them in an arrangement that lightness is needed at the top and around the edge of the arrangement, with the longer flowers throughout the arrangement and the heavier flowers nearer the centre.

If you have bunchy flowers grouped one way in an arrangement and single ones in the opposite direction, you will find that you need more single flowers to balance the multi-headed ones. When using single flowers try to get as much variation of shape as possible.

Choice of foliage

This needs as much thought as the choosing of flowers. Single leaves have various shapes. They can be broad and rounded such as the bergenia; oval and pointed like the hosta; heart-shaped like the leaf of the arum lily; irregular like the *Begonia rex*; or have a serrated edge like the artichoke. These leaves can be used to give heart to an arrangement especially when spiky flowers are incorporated. Their

Among the many different shapes and sizes of single leaves for flower arranging is the bergenia (above), whilst a useful compound leaf is the Senecio greyii *(top). There are also a variety of tall thin leaves, such as the sansevieria (right), which are usually placed upright in an arrangement as they normally grow this way.*

good contrast to provide interest and balance or try to blend them with the flowers to provide a different impact. If the flowers are fussy, select a clean-cut foliage. If, however, the flowers are single, a more fussy foliage can be used.

Lastly, there are the tall thin leaves such as sansevieria and reeds. Since these grow naturally upright, they should be positioned reasonably vertically. This type of leaf is valuable for establishing the height of an arrangement. Do not make a fan of them as this can look particularly ugly. Ferns can be used upright in an arrangement or sideways along the edge as both ways will emulate their natural habitat.

Grasses

These will add lightness and interest to an arrangement, and many seedsmen offer a wide variety of ornamental grasses from which you can make a selection if you want to grow some of the many different forms in your garden. Some of the ornamental grasses are very large and can be useful for quite large arrangements, while dainty grasses look attractive in smaller ones. Grasses can also be dried and used in the winter. As with tall thin leaves, grasses should be arranged in an upright position.

Twigs and branches

These are very useful for giving shape to a line arrangement and for providing interest in a mass arrangement.

Lichen is often found on branches of fir trees but if you can find it on less brittle wood these pieces can be stored for several years without disintegrating. When placing lichen-covered branches into an arrangement, the portion of the stem which is to go under water should be scraped free of lichen as this will siphon water out of the container.

Alder trees are generally found beside rivers, ponds, lakes and other damp habitats and in winter and spring the twigs with their small cones and catkins are extremely attractive. The catkins do not produce their pollen until spring but they are still excellent for winter decoration.

This line arrangement shows how alder branches – cut before the catkin buds

Below left: Lichen-covered branches are useful for line arrangements and add interest to arrangements of mixed flowers. If used at Christmas, they can be glittered for the occasion.

Below: Grasses, either fresh or dried, add lightness to an arrangement. When dried they often turn an attractive golden shade.

have opened – can be used. The base for the arrangement is a woven tray, and on this has been placed, slightly to the left of centre, a small metal container in which is placed a large pinholder. Used with the branches are nine orange tulips, the variety being Apeldoorn, and five bergenia leaves which have a slight orange tinge to them. Five pinky-orange pebbles help cover the dish and give added interest.

First establish the outline with the alder, choosing a reasonably straight piece as the first and longest stem, although a slight curve away from the centre at the top is an advantage. Secure this three-quarters of the way back on the pinholder in the centre. If this branch has another attached to it this may be considered as the second or third stem at the back of the arrangement depending on the length of the attached twig. Next position the second or third branch close to the first or both if the first branch had no convenient side twigs. The natural curve of these branches should be away from the centre. The width is established by placing a piece of alder low on either side, the left side piece extending a little more over the tray than the right side. Have these pieces close to the tray to ensure that the arrangement and tray become one unit visually. It is nicer not to have a too symmetrical arrangement, which is why the container is not in the centre of the tray. The overall width should be slightly less than the height. Position a piece of alder in the front. Finish the outline shape by placing pieces of alder between the main outline ones, decreasing the lengths of the stems quite sharply at the back. Do not hide too much

of the tray, so have a broken line around the edge.

Next place in the tulips. Stem length permitting, have the smallest tulip at the top, placing the stem close to the longest alder and curving it in the same direction as the branch. A second tulip with a larger flower but shorter stem should be positioned to the left side of the first, and a third flower, larger and shorter-stemmed still, on the other side. Each should be secured progressively a little further forward on the pinholder.

Now choose a small flower and secure this low at the front near the front stem of alder, placing its stem sideways on to the pinholder. A second tulip with a larger flower and shorter stem should be positioned to the right of this front flower with a third, larger and shorter-stemmed, to the left of the front flower. These last two flowers are slightly higher than the first flower at the front.

Then, in the centre, place three tulips to join the back and front groups together. A small, reasonably long-stemmed flower should be placed in a line with the flowers at the centre back and front. A larger, shorter-stemmed flower goes to the right of this one, further back on the pinholder with an even larger but shorter-stemmed flower to the left of centre and towards the front. The tulips should be roughly equidistant.

The five bergenia leaves are needed to give added weight in the centre and to frame the flowers, and these are positioned next. Place a small but long-stemmed leaf at the back near the first tulip and reaching to about halfway up its stem. Another small leaf with a longish

Line drawings illustrating a line arrangement using alder branches, nine tulips and five bergenia leaves. The first diagram shows the shape established by the alder branches, the second more alder on the outline and the placement of the nine tulips. The third diagram shows the five leaves in position and the fourth is a side view showing how the arrangement is built up with both alder and tulips, from the tallest flower at the top to the longest at the front.

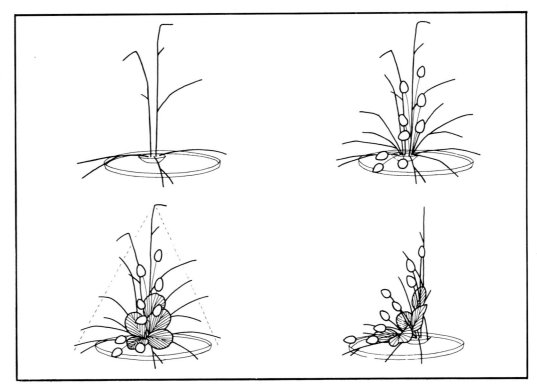

stem goes against the first flower at the front edge, but it is better to keep it shorter than the tulip. A third, shorter leaf is placed to the right of the first, with a fourth of similar size to the left of the second. The fifth and largest leaf should be cut short and placed sideways in the centre of the arrangement.

Add the finishing touches by placing a few alder branches attractively between the tulips, and if any of the pinholder or container can be seen, use some tulip leaves to cover them and also to fill in at the back of the arrangement.

The completed line arrangement on a round woven tray with a small metal dish holding the pinholder. A few pebbles are placed on the tray for added interest.

23

Arrange the pebbles from the edge of the tray towards the container so the eye is drawn towards the centre.

While the alder is useful in the winter and spring, lime tree bracts are ideal for summer use. The bracts develop in high summer though these might not be readily noticed when the tree is in full leaf. If you are lucky enough to have access to a tree you can judiciously cut off some of the elegant stems. Trim away the leaves to reveal the lime green bracts. You could use the stripped lime prepared in this way in both mass and line arrangements. The lime bracts can also be preserved for winter use as explained in a later chapter.

Hazelnut catkins are firm favourites with flower arrangers and most attractive when combined with daffodils. Another catkin-bearing tree is the willow and one species has the additional interest of contorted branches. Pleasing arrangements can be achieved with just a few catkin

branches and a group of large leaves beneath to cover the mechanics. The pretty branches of daphne are very beautiful in association with just a few flowers which pick up the colour of the daphne. *Hammamelis mollis* is another good early flowering shrub as is *Chimonanthes fragrans* and *Viburnum fragrans*.

Many other beautiful wood subjects can be found in garden and countryside. Do be sure when cutting twigs from a shrub or tree that you do it very carefully so as not to spoil the overall shape of the plant.

Bulrushes

These give the flower arranger another interesting shape, and used at the top of an arrangement at differing lengths can be very attractive. I like the natural-coloured ones rather than the dyed, but these also have their uses for festive occasions.

Opposite page: A simple all-round arrangement in a green pottery bowl. A round of florists' foam is placed in the centre with wire netting over it. In the container are branches of Hamamelis mollis *and* Mahonia aquifolia *foliage. The outline was established around the edge first as with a basic all-round arrangement. The hamamelis is grouped from one side to the opposite side of the bowl and is the tallest flower in the centre. The mahonia foliage links with the brown colour in the centre of the hamamelis flowers.*

Bulrushes can add a pointed shape to arrangements. It is nicer to use them upright as they grow this way. The preserved ones are useful in the winter.

Dried seedheads such as poppy and teasel are good to use in the autumn and winter. Seedheads can also be used when they are fresh.

Berries and seedheads

Invaluable for autumn arrangements, they can be used on their own with just a little foliage or combined with both flowers and foliage. There are many varieties of berries in a wide range of colours, so it is quite easy to match a particular flower with a berry. Heavier sprays of berries can be kept to the centre of an arrangement and can be used as a focal point. Lighter branches can be grouped throughout. If necessary clip some of the leaves off the branches to show the berries more clearly, but it is better not to completely defoliate them.

How many flowers?

It is very difficult for a beginner to determine how many flowers are needed for a mass arrangement. This depends on the size of the container, where the arrangement is to be placed and the size of the flowers. Guidance in this respect is not easy, but as an example a medium-sized urn with a facing arrangement would need roughly 40 flowers. The right

judgement comes with experience and with becoming accustomed to certain sized containers. You will be able to tell by eye the number of flowers you will need when cutting them from the garden or buying from the florist.

The amount of foliage will vary with how many flowers are being used; more will be needed for a large arrangement with a limited number of flowers.

If you are to have less than 12 flowers in an arrangement, keep to an uneven number. As has been mentioned, when using a small number of flowers in the centre of an arrangement the placement can look regimented – so too can the flowers if using an even number when they are being grouped through an arrangement. This also applies to leaves.

Flowers with their own foliage

It will look more natural if the foliage of the flowers to be arranged can also be used, in which case group it through with the flower to which it belongs. Leave compound leaves of roses attached to a section of the main stem. This helps to secure them into the arrangement. Tulip leaves are sometimes rather large and heavy. To overcome this, they can be cut short and the cut ends rolled round pieces of stem which will help to hold them in the netting. Daffodil leaves are very attractive when used with their own flowers. Bunches of three or five are more effective especially if each leaf in the bunch is placed at a different length. It is better to keep them shorter than the flowers. Dahlia foliage is good but it should receive hot water treatment before being arranged. Peonies, too, have long-lasting leaves and turn an attractive colour in the autumn. These should be cut leaving a piece of main stem attached as for roses. These are just a few examples of flowers which can be used with their own leaves.

Fruit and vegetables

These may seem somewhat strange items to use in flower arranging, but it is astonishing how effective they can look with flowers and foliage or even just foliage. You can use a selection of fruit and/or vegetables or just one kind. They really are tremendous fun to arrange. The most popular fruit with flowers are probably grapes, as they seem to go as well with many kinds of flowers in simple one-variety flower arrangements as with mixed arrangements. Choose whichever colour grapes enhance the flowers to their best advantage.

This arrangement is a simple one using green grapes, sansevieria leaves, bergenia leaves and orange tiger lilies. The container is a green plate on which is placed a metal container holding a large pinholder.

Position the rectangular plate so that the longest side is facing the front and position the container in the centre near the back of the plate. Arrange the fruit first. The grapes need to be wired with florists' stub wires to make sure they are held firmly in the arrangement. Make a hook with the wire and place it over the stem of the grapes, then twist it around the stem and attach it to the pinholder so the grapes are resting on the plate to the left of the centre. The three sansevieria leaves establish the tallest point at the back. These graduate down to the left. The three tiger lilies are placed in next, one going high to the right of the tallest sansevieria leaf, the second low to the right to balance the grapes, and the third midway between these two and slightly to the left. Lilies need to be handled carefully to avoid the pollen from the stamens staining the petals. The stamens

can be removed, but the flowers then look a little unnatural. Five bergenia leaves are positioned as follows: one small one towards the back, a second small one low to the right of the grapes, another slightly shorter to the left and lifting up towards the centre, one to the right of the centre and turned sideways, and the fifth, which is fairly large and short stemmed, to the left and behind the tallest bergenia leaf at the back.

The bergenia and sansevieria leaves give the arrangement clean-cut lines and lend a refreshing look to complement the exotic mood created by the grapes and lilies. The margins of the sansevieria leaves also pick up the colour of the grapes.

On the green plate is an arrangement of grapes with three orange lilies, three sanseviera leaves and five bergenia leaves. The material is used in a small dish which contains a pinholder. How to prepare the arrangement is described in detail in this chapter.

This arrangement in a wicker trough, using bun moss with flowers placed in bunches as if they are growing, can be used as an informal table-centre arrangement. The pictures illustrate the progress of the arrangement in three stages, the first showing the bun moss placed on the wire netting with some daffodils in two places. In the second picture the two bunches of daffodils are complete and hyacinths have been placed at one end and Helleborus niger *at the other.*

The leaves borne on the flowering stems of the tiger lilies can make interesting additions to such an arrangement. The pieces of stem left after cutting the lily stems shorter are well clothed in leaves. Disguise the cut end by trimming at an angle so that it cannot be seen and use these leaves through the arrangement and to cover the pinholder.

Other fruit and vegetables which are attractive for their colouring include apples of various colours, pears, pineapples, peaches, cauliflowers, aubergines, peppers, artichokes and indeed any fruit or vegetables which will go well with certain colouring of flowers and also

the containers being used. Pineapples and peaches go exceptionally well with copper or brass and with flowers of apricot colouring. Indeed a pineapple looks very dramatic in arrangements with its lovely spray of leaves on the top. Aubergines are attractive with pink flowers. One could go on forever thinking of combinations and I am sure you will have great delight in selecting them for yourself.

When choosing a selection, the shapes of the fruit and vegetbles must also be taken into consideration – in the same way that different shaped flowers have to be selected for mixed flower arrangements – the large round fruit or vegetable in the centre with the smaller oval or long-shaped fruits and vegetables going to the sides and some even higher towards the back of the arrangement. Often it can be more effective to have spiky kinds of flowers with the more solid varieties of fruit and vegetables and larger, more clean-cut flowers with fruit which has several smaller fruits on a main stem. There are endless possibilities.

Mosses

Mosses are useful in various ways in arrangements. The green bun or carpet moss can be used to cover wire netting with bunches of flowers placed in the gaps of the moss, as described at the end of this chapter. It can be used in line arrangements to cover a pinholder. Lichen or reindeer moss, which is the grey-coloured moss often found under heather on moors in certain countries, is also useful in line arrangements. It can be bought in its dried state and when soaked becomes spongy. For festive occasions it is a useful decoration as it can be used dry and sprayed with various coloured paints. It can also be used to cover a container, to make a base for arranging bunches of flowers.

The following arrangement uses bun moss. The container is a wicker trough with a plastic lining. Two small pinholders are placed a little way from the side at either end where the taller flowers are to be positioned. Wire netting goes into the container and is raised slightly higher than usual so that, when the moss is placed on it, this does not touch the water. The plant materials used are 18 white daffodils, nine stems of *Helleborus niger* (Christmas rose), five stems of blue hyacinth, two bunches of violets, white erica (heather) and several pieces of trailing ivy.

The arrangement is seen from all sides. Place bun moss on the netting, leaving a few spaces into which the flowers are to be positioned. The flowers are placed in bunches for a natural effect. The two groups of daffodils with their leaves are placed first and secured on pinholders, one group being taller than the other and both groups having stems of various lengths. Other flowers are placed in at the ends of the basket, two hyacinth on one side and three hellebore at the opposite end, all these being low on the container to connect the arrangement to the basket. Slightly further down the side of the container place a group of hyacinth near the hellebore, and another group of hellebore near the hyacinth at the opposite end, with a bunch in the centre between the daffodils. Loosen the bunches of violets and place a bunch on either side of the basket. The heather and ivy trails can also be placed on both sides. The finished arrangement looks like a spring garden.

The picture on the left shows the completed arrangement, with more hyacinths and hellebores added, as well as ivy, violets and heather. The arrangement is described in this chapter.

4 Equipment Used in Flower Arranging

It is well worth buying special equipment if you are doing many flower arrangements, as it makes it much easier with the proper tools.

Flower scissors Specially designed flower scissors are available and are essential equipment for the arranger. They incorporate two useful features – a serrated edge which is useful for cutting heavy stems, and a wire-cutting groove.

Secateurs These are needed for the really thick stems where flower scissors are not heavy enough. When doing exceptionally large arrangements and using flowering tree branches, they are often essential.

Candlecups These are small containers which are designed to fit on to candlesticks. They are available in various sizes and can also be fitted into the necks of bottles, which make appropriate containers for parties, and in other narrow-necked containers. Candlecups are made in chrome, brass and copper and in white or coloured plastic and are inexpensive. Although they can be used for facing arrangements, especially when they are arranged in narrow-necked vases, they are particularly ideal for all-round arrangements. If you are arranging a three-branched candelabra, either fit a candlecup on each side and leave the centre free, or have one candlecup in the centre and leave the two sides free, as if you arranged all three the result would be rather heavy. When using a candlecup for an all-round arrangement a candle can be included in the centre, as can be seen by the candlestick arrangement described here.

This candlecup arrangement was a brass candlestick with a brass candlecup to match which has been attached to the candlestick with a reusable adhesive, such as Bostik Blu-Tack. In the candlecup is wire netting which is tied into it with silver reel wire. A larger space is left in the netting in the centre to allow the candle to be placed in more easily. Florists' foam could be used instead of netting. The candle is green in keeping with the mixed green foliage with a few green flowers, and is placed in first. The arrangement is an all-round one and has many varieties of leaves in it, but even though it is very mixed one still needs to group from one side to the other even if only three pieces of one particular foliage are being used.

The main seven outline points are placed in first. These are the same length from the rim of the candlecup to the tip of the leaf or flower, and are two ericas and one each of euonymus, variegated rue, hebe, escallonia and rosemary. Place leaves of varying lengths fairly close to the candle, but not touching it. These are kept lower than the tallest flowers in the centre of a basic all-round arrangement, as the candle gives necessary height. Next place pieces in between the outline at different lengths, making sure the outline is kept round but with a broken line. Position flowers and leaves through-

A selection of equipment frequently used by the flower arranger. Included are florists' foam, wire netting, tubes, pinholders, candlecup, candle holders, silver reel wire and the all-important scissors.

This arrangement in a candlecup on a brass candlestick is an adaptation from the basic all-round arrangement and is described in this chapter. It is in various shades of green and has foliage of many different shapes. The flower buds of the heather and the green Helleborus foetidus *flowers fit in with the overall colour scheme.*

Below: A tube or cone being attached to a green square stick with transparent sticky tape. These are used to hold flower stems which are not sufficiently long to achieve the height required for large arrangements.

out the arrangement. The other flowers besides the erica are the green hellebore (*Helleborus foetidus*), and other leaves included are ivies, scindapsus and tradescantia. Although the arrangement is low, some pieces need to be a little longer to get the variation of stem length. Cover the netting with shorter pieces of foliage.

Cones or tubes Although these are seldom needed for arrangements in the home, they are excellent when creating pedestal arrangements in churches or for receptions. They are used to give extra length to stems when it is impossible to obtain flowers with long enough stems to achieve the correct proportions in large arrangements.

First attach the cone to a green-painted square stick with transparent sticky tape so that cone and stick overlap by about 75 mm (3 inches). A square stick is better than a round one because a round one will tend to twist in the netting, whereas a square one will hold its position. The length of the stick depends on the height of the arrangement and the length of the flower stems. For a pedestal arrangement three cones are usually sufficient but in a really vast arrangement as many as 20 could be used. This, however, is exceptional.

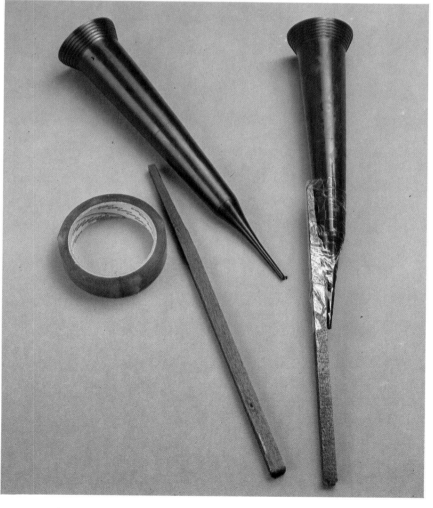

A pinholder is used in the centre of this round green pottery bowl in order to hold a line arrangement of Viburnum fragrans *twigs, three pink hyacinths, and three* Begonia rex *leaves, which have been chosen to pick up the colour of the pink flowers. The outline of twigs is established first. Next the three hyacinths are positioned, the tallest one with the smallest flower going at the back, another, shorter, one to the right and further forward on the pinholder, and a third to the left, again shorter nd further forward still on the pinholder. The* Begonia rex *leaves are so placed as to cover the pinholder, with the largest turned sideways near the centre of the bowl, a smaller one coming over the rim of the bowl on the left and, facing it, a third one at the back.*

Wire netting This is a wire mesh, which can be bought by length, used for holding flowers in a container. The diameter of the mesh does vary but the 50-mm (2-inch) is preferable to the smaller meshes. If the larger mesh is difficult to obtain, use the smaller mesh, but use a little less of it. The 50-mm (2-inch) is preferable because it can be rolled tighter if needed for thinner-stemmed flowers and there is more space, if loosely rolled, for larger stems without damaging them. You will learn by trial and error how much is required for a certain container. This varies with the type of flower to be used and the thickness of stems. On the whole the stems of spring flowers are thicker than those produced the rest of the year, so less netting will be needed then. The wire netting must be firmly secured in the vase otherwise you are unlikely to achieve a successful arrangement. This is explained fully in Chapter 7 on the methods of holding flowers in a container.

Pinholders One of the most useful aids to flower arrangements, they are available in different sizes and shapes, and can be round, oblong or crescent-shaped. You can buy pinholders with the spikes close together, or further apart if you are arranging heavier-stemmed flowers and foliage. It is worth paying the extra cost of a heavy-based pinholder as this will be more stable for a line arrangement. The lighter-weight ones can be secured with a reusable adhesive, such as Bostik Blu-tack, or plasticine but they are never quite as firm. Pinholders can be used under wire netting in an arrangement as explained in Chapter 7.

Florists' foam This is a water-retaining substance. There are several types of it on the market, probably the best known in Britain being Oasis. It needs to be thoroughly soaked so that when the stems of the flowers are anchored into it, they do not meet any dry patches. The florists' foam can be cut wet or dry to the required size for the container. Unfortunately it is more costly than wire netting because it cannot be used indefinitely. After it has been used for three or four arrangements it crumbles and will not grip the stems. How to use florists' foam in various containers and arrangements is described in Chapter 7.

Dry florists' foam This is used for dried or artificial arrangements, as it holds them more firmly than ordinary florists' foam. It is never soaked so cannot be used for fresh flowers. It is ideal for silk flower arrangements, and for festive occasion arrangements using various artificial materials. It is useful for all dried or preserved flowers and foliage.

Holders for florists' foam These are useful when the foam is used on its own. Although similar to a pinholder, they only have about six spikes which are each about 32 mm (1¼ inches) high. The foam is placed on these spikes and is held firmly by them. They are useful when using heavier branches because the extra weight at the base helps to balance the branch. As an added precaution they could be attached to the container with a reusable adhesive, such as Bostik Blu-tack, or plasticine. Dry florists' foam can also be used on them.

Gravel Sometimes when large heavy plant materials are used in a container which is relatively light, the arrangement can become unstable and topple. This should not happen if the finished arrangement is correctly balanced but you might run into difficulties making it up. Gravel or even sand can be placed in the bottom of the container to make it heavier. The gravel will not harm the flowers and will not take up too much room in the container.

Pedestals These are the stands which hold the flower container when doing very large arrangements or groups of flowers for receptions and churches or where an extra large arrangement is required. When using flat, relatively light bowls on pedestals, these should if possible be attached to their stands with string or thick reel wire to hold them firmly in position. When the container is heavier and urn-shaped this is not necessary. With a pedestal arrangement in a marquee, it is advisable to anchor it well as the ground is more uneven and it could topple. If a wrought-iron stand is to be used, this can be staked to the ground. Pedestals or plinths can be made of wrought-iron, wood, marble, etc.

Reusable adhesive or plasticine This can be used to anchor the pinholder onto a dish, although if the pinholder is sufficiently heavy and the flowers are well balanced, it may not be necessary to use it. If the arrangement has to be carried to an exhibition or competition then it is an added precaution, to hold it steady. Best not to use it on metal containers such as silver, copper or brass. A popular make of reusable adhesive in Britain is Bostik Blu-tack which is easily obtainable.

Reels of silver wire Lengths of silver and also black wire, similar to fuse wire, come on reels and are of various thicknesses. It is used for tying wire netting into containers, though if it is unobtainable then thin string could be used instead. The 30- and 32-gauge wire is the most useful.

Stub wires Sometimes called florists' wires, they can be used for attaching fruit into a container and also to give some dried flower heads an artificial stem. They are sold by the bundle.

Sticky tape This can be used for attaching wire netting to certain containers such as pottery but it is not advisable to stick it to brass, copper, silver or similar metal containers as it can spoil the surface. Also use it to attach sticks to cones.

Sprayer It is a good idea to have a mist sprayer, as often flowers benefit by spraying overhead, especially flowers which take a large proportion of moisture through their petals such as violets and hydrangeas. Also when bun moss is used it does not get any moisture from the container so it needs a spray overhead to keep it green and fresh.

Watering can A small watering can with a long spout for easy filling of containers is useful. There are many available on the market ranging from brass to plastic. A teapot with a fairly long spout is an excellent substitute!

Dust sheets These are essential when doing arrangements for receptions and churches. They not only keep the floor clean but make tidying up so much easier and quicker. They are also very convenient when doing flowers in the home. I find the thick material ones preferable to plastic sheeting as the latter can get slippery and can be quite dangerous.

Candle holders These hold candles into place in arrangements such as table centres. A candle holder has spikes in its base to attach it securely into florist's foam or a pinholder.

A selection of equipment used at various times when flower arranging. The items include a watering can, a mist sprayer, dry florists' foam, stub or florists' wires and secateurs.

5 Containers Used for Flower Arrangements

Opposite page: The silver tazza used here has a shallow bowl held by three dolphins. It is arranged simply with white freesia and variegated ivy trails, as a basic facing arrangement. The height and the overall width are each approximately one and a half times the height of the container.

Below: A selection of containers for the flower arranger. At the back is a heavy pottery vase for facing arrangements, to the right of it a bamboo vase for simple facing arrangements. The shallow pottery bowl at the front and the oval pottery trough can be used for various arrangements.

Deciding on which of the many containers available to choose for a particular arrangement is very difficult, as the final decision can either make or completely spoil an arrangement. Points to look out for are the suitability of the flowers and foliage to the container, the shape of the container in relation to the proposed shape of the arrangement, and the position of the finished arrangement in a room. Here are some different shaped containers with ideas as to how and where they can be used.

Tazza This elegant container is probably the most useful of all. It is wide but shallow and is mounted on a stem which always gives an air of grace. The wider the top of the container, the easier it is to place the stems of the flowers when doing an arrangement, one of the reasons why a beginner should start with a tazza first. Being shallow, the tazza needs to be kept topped up with water.

Tazzas are easily obtainable and are made in many materials. Alabaster ones are particularly lovely but they do need to have a metal lining or a shallow dish of appropriate size placed into them. There are tazzas in silver, brass, copper, pewter, glass and a great variety of porcelain and pottery ones. A tazza is versatile, suitable for all kinds of flowers and lends itself to many arrangements either for the centre of a table or for symmetrical and asymmetrical facing arrangements against a wall.

Bowls Although not as elegant as tazzas as they do not have a stem, nevertheless bowls are extremely useful. They are attractive containers for low all-round arrangements for the centre of a table. Used like this they are often known as posy bowls. They successfully accommodate symmetrical and asymmetrical facing arrangements. Large bowls are often used in pedestal arrangements – a mixing bowl, painted in a colour to match the pedestal, will do admirably. It is surprising how often kitchen bowls double up for flower arranging to save the expense of buying a special container. Again as with tazzas, bowls can be obtained in silver, brass, copper, glass, pottery, porcelain, etc., so there is a wide choice.

Urns They are usually tall and fairly narrow and as such are very graceful. They are great favourites with flower arrangers even though they are more difficult to arrange because of their limited width, and extra care needs to be taken when using them. They are only really suitable for facing arrangements, and I think a symmetrical one looks nicer in them than an asymmetrical. All-round arrangements never seem to look comfortable in them because of the urn's height and width. This shape of vase looks attractive in a niche. Urns are again

manufactured in a variety of materials including bronze, copper, brass, silver, pewter, alabaster, porcelain and pottery.

The arrangement described here is in a grey pottery urn and has a collection of clashing red flowers. These are the reds which include the blue-reds and the yellow-reds, as is described in Chapter 10. As the container is relatively thin and deep, only wire netting is placed in, which will be sufficient to secure the stems of the plant material. How to put the netting into the container is described in Chapter 7. Florists' foam could be used if preferred.

The collection of flowers chosen are 15 stems of blue-red kaffir lilies, nine orange montbretia, two stems of red spray chrysanthemums, five dark red dahlias, three pieces of mountain spinach, three pieces of pyracantha with orange-red berries, three stems of wild rose hips, three pieces of bryony, three pieces of honeysuckle berries and three stems of skimmia berries. The foliage is in autumnal shades: seven stems of prunus and five pieces of *Ajuga repens atropurpurea*. There are also three bergenia leaves for the centre.

Commence the arrangement by placing a stem of montbretia, which is about twice the height of the container, three-quarters of the way back in the centre of the container. Place a shorter-stemmed kaffir lily to the right of this and another montbretia to the left. These three flowers should be close together, so secure them through the same hole in the netting. Each should be a slightly different length. Next establish the width by placing a montbretia with a curved stem low down on the right-hand side, three-quarters of the way back in the container. The stem of the flower should be fairly short so that the completed arrangement echoes the elegant shape of the urn. On the opposite side, place a kaffir lily which is the same length as the montbretia on the right-hand side. Another montbretia should be

Above and right: A facing arrangement using clashing red flowers in an urn. The flowers and foliage are montbretia (A), kaffir lilies (B), dahlias (C), bergenia (D), chrysanthemum (E), pyracantha (F), bryony (G), skimmia (H), prunus (J), hips (K), mountain spinach (L), honeysuckle (M) and ajuga (N).

Opposite page: A brown ovenware dish is here used for a line arrangmeent with two bulrushes, three stems of red spray chrysanthemums, three red-coloured croton leaves and a few stems of Mahonia aquifolia *foliage.*

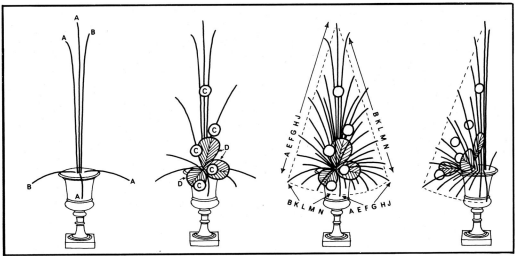

brought well out over the front of the urn in line with the tallest flower at the back. The main outline flowers are now in position; all the subsequent stems should appear to radiate from the tallest flower at the back. This is a little more difficult with a narrow-necked vase.

Next position the dahlias, the main flowers in the centre. A fairly small dahlia is placed high but centred in the arrangement, with another small flower to the left of the centre at the front. Zigzag the other dahlias to meet up with these two flowers but keep them fairly close through the centre. The three bergenia leaves are placed to frame the dahlias. One should go over the edge at the front to the left of the centre; another, the largest, turned sideways in the centre, and the third is placed at the back in the arrangement facing the one at the front.

Go back to the outline at this stage and introduce the berries into the arrangement, and place some plant material between the main outline points. Graduate the length of stems down quite sharply at the back edge to avoid a rounded top. Create a good semi-circle around the front edge. The group of flowers and foliage going from high on the left to low on the right are montbretia, chrysanthemum with the berries of the pyracantha, bryony and skimmia, and prunus foliage. In the opposite direction are the kaffir lilies, rose hips, mountain spinach, honeysuckle berries and ajuga foliage. Place some of each kind of flower and berry on the outline, keeping particularly curved stems like those of the bryony at the front of the arrangement and lower down. The straight-stemmed rose hips look well at the back, and any of the curved stems of the hips should go low on the left-hand front.

At this stage place some foliage to cover the netting. Connect up the groups of flowers, berries and foliage and, remembering to turn some of the plant material slightly sideways to keep the arrangement looking more natural, place them throughout the arrangement. When there are only three pieces of a particular flower to be used, as there are in several cases in this arrangement, have one high at the back, one low over the opposite edge and one in the centre. Try to have plenty of variation of stem length and merge the groups of flowers through. Check that all the netting is covered.

Troughs These are long and low containers and can be many different sizes. They can be used for a variety of arrangements and look exceptionally good for table centres, especially for long tables at formal dinners. They look well on mantel-

pieces, windowsills and shelves and are excellent containers for arrangements on church windowsills and at the chancel steps. Symmetrical and asymmetrical facing arrangements can be long and low in keeping with their shape or can be quite tall, depending on the positions in which they are to be placed. L-shaped arrangements are also a suitable shape to arrange in them. Wide troughs are particularly useful for line arrangements.

Troughs are made of various materials such as china, copper, brass, silver, pottery, wrought iron and basketwork, providing a wide choice when selecting a trough for a particular type of flower.

Cylindrical containers This a popular shape for a home with modern décor. It is not the easiest shape to arrange because of the narrow opening at the top, but with the right plant material it can look sensational. It is usually not as suitable for a traditional setting in a room furnished with antiques, but in certain circumstances the two can be blended successfully together. An arrangement in a cylinder is attractive when it is kept very tall and thin, in keeping with the shape of the container. Cylinders are manufactured in a variety of materials, including porcelain, pottery and brass, and also come in natural bamboo.

Oval containers These can be either a shallow oval dish or an oval container with a stem. Either way an oval container is useful for a table centre and looks especially lovely on an oval table. If the dish is not on a stem it is suitable for an L-shaped arrangement, and if the dish is low and fairly shallow it is suitable for a line arrangement. It will also hold a symmetrical or asymmetrical facing arrangement, but if the container is on a stem it is better to keep the arrangement lower than a basic facing arrangement. These oval containers are obtainable in glass, porcelain, pottery, etc.

Baskets These can be found in a variety of shapes and when made of china or glass are most attractive for more formal arrangements. When they are fashioned out of basketwork they are especially suited to country-type flowers and informal arrangements, but they do require water-tight linings. If they do not have one inside when they are purchased, baking tins can be used successfully. These will need to be painted in order to seal them so use a colour to match the basketwork. It is preferable to have a matt finish paint as this is less conspicuous than gloss. Another good lining is a plastic container, available in many sizes and colours. All one has to do is remove the lid; they do not have to be painted and are quite strong. This inside container needs to be level with the rim of the basket, so may need padding beneath. Baskets with handles are extremely popular and there is a great range available both in size and shape from the plain rectangular to the prettier shaped ones. The trug basket is very attractive, especially a small-sized one, but is more difficult to use than other baskets because of the low handle which needs to be seen after the flowers have been arranged. Facing arrangements and table centres are suitable arrangements for baskets with handles.

Very pretty arrangements can be created in baskets with lids but these baskets are not quite as useful as those with handles as they are unsuitable for all-round arrangements. It is better not to cover all the lid with flowers and foliage.

Basketwork troughs also have their uses especially for simple arrangements using bun moss with bunches of flowers placed in between. L-shaped arrangements are also particularly attractive in them.

Small china and glass baskets are pretty arranged with dainty flowers and foliage, especially for a bedroom arrangement. Silver cake baskets are good as table centres for a dinner or luncheon party.

Shells When arranging flowers in these containers, try to keep the shape of the

Above: A selection of containers. The urn at the rear is in dull green which is a useful colour for many flowers. The dolphin on the left is attractive for asymmetrical arrangements and easier to use than the narrow-necked vase on the right. In the foreground is a basket with a handle which is suitable for country-type arrangements.

Right: A candlecup placed on a narrow-necked vase can be attached with silver reel wire or a reusable adhesive such as Bostik Blu-tack round the edge to hold it in position. The candlecup gives more space in which to arrange flowers and enables them to come horizontally over the edge of the container more easily.

shell. This usually results in long, low arrangements. Real seashore shells can also be used, though they sometimes have to be made stable by using adhesive or plasticine on the base. Florists' foam can be used in gaps in the shell to provide a support for the flowers. Check carefully that the water does not leak from it before placing the shell on a polished surface.

Narrow-necked containers These include the narrow-necked altar vases found in many churches. They are extremely difficult to arrange because there is only room for perhaps two or three stems in their necks. To overcome this secure a candlecup in the neck with silver wire or a reusable adhesive, such as Bos-

tik Blu-tack. Alternatively a funnel, which has been plugged with a cork to stop the water running through, can be used in the same way.

Wall vases Wall vases are most frequently made of china, but can also be made of metal materials. Second-hand silver meat covers can be cut in two and metal placed across the opening at the back and made watertight. When mounted on a wall they can look beautiful with pretty flowing plant material arranged in them.

Plates and flat dishes These are used a great deal for line arrangements. A small metal container needs to be placed on the dish to hold the water, mechanics, flowers

A basic facing arrangement using a narrow-necked vase with a candlecup attached in which there is florists' foam with wire netting over it. The flowers used are pale pink carnation sprays, cream daffodils, pink roses and cream carnations. The foliage is variegated ivy and euonymus with three single ivy leaves in the centre.

Wall vases are a change from the more usual containers. This one is made of white pottery and is completed as a basic asymmetrical arrangement. The flowers are in pink and red with grey foliage. The plant material grouped from high on the right to low on the left consists of nine pink carnations, leycesteria berries and eucalyptus foliage, and going the opposite way are five dark red roses and variegated ivy. In the centre are three pink hyacinths with three Begonia rex *leaves. It is helpful to have plant material with curved stems to obtain a flowing look to the arrangement.*

and foliage. Meat plates, if deep enough, are very good for arranging natural-looking gardens with bun moss and plant materials.

Other containers Some containers can be used which were not originally meant to hold flowers. Many Victorian *objets d'art* can be converted. Needlework, writing and Bible boxes have great potential and can become favourites for flower arrangements. To convert and arrange a writing box, first one needs to have a water-tight lining – a baking tin which has been painted with matt paint is ideal. In this box the lining is placed on blocks of wood so that its top edge is level with the top of the box; otherwise, it is difficult to get a good flow of flowers over the edge of the box. The lid of the box makes a good background to the flowers and can be attractively lined with material to tone with the flowers, and part of it should be seen in the completed arrangement.

Pieces of wood cut to fit inside the lid can be covered with different coloured and textured materials and attached by transparent sticky tape. In this way a range can be built up so that the appropriate colour and texture is available for whatever flowers and foliage are being used. The material also needs to look correct against the particular wood of the box – satinwood and velvet look well with shiny woods.

In this particular arrangement a creamy yellow colouring is used so choose a cream-coloured lining for the lid of the box. The arrangement is going to be L-shaped so that part of the lid on the right can be seen. If one wished, the flowers could be arranged higher in the centre so that the two top corners could be seen or the lid could be half closed and the flowers arranged to spill out from under it. The flowers used here are cream broom, five cream stock, 11 single cream tulips, three

double yellow tulips and nine yellow roses, three straw-coloured hyacinth, three polyanthus and one bunch of the yellow Cheerfulness narcissi. The foliage and flowers for filling in are golden philadelphus (*Philadelphus coronaruis aureus*), spurge (euphorbia) and three bergenia leaves.

A pinholder is placed in the left-hand side of the box towards the back, and wire netting placed in the container as described in Chapter 7. Three pieces of broom of differing lengths establishes the height and then a stem of stock is placed fairly high near the centre of the broom. The overall width needs to be roughly equal to the height. One of the smaller-flowered stock is used to mark the width on the right-hand side, being placed so that it comes well out over the edge of the box. A rose is used as the outline point on the left-hand side but not as far over the edge as on the right-hand side. A narcissus becomes the longest flower over the front edge in line with the tallest flower at the back. Return to the height and place a rose to the right side of the stock and a tulip the other side of it. The arrangement is filled in by grouping the single tulips, stock and broom high on the left to low on the right, with the roses and narcissi grouped the opposite way. The flowers are brought well out over the edge. The stems radiate from the pieces of broom at the back. The hyacinths, double tulips and polyanthus are placed in near the centre. Cover the netting with the spurge and have some of it coming over the edge of the box. The philadelphus is high on the left side and low on the right, with some covering the netting. Place the bergenia leaves near the centre with the hyacinth. Check that the netting is covered and that the flowers are distributed fairly evenly throughout the arrangement, making sure that part of the lid is visible.

Other objects that can be converted for use in flower arrangements are Victorian oil lamps. Remove the wick and replace it with a candlecup. Glass oil lamps look beautiful with matching flowers but lamps can be found made of china, silver and gilt. Arrangements can be all-round or facing, but if the lamp is very tall it will look better with a facing arrangement.

Silver meat covers make splendid flower containers. Their conversion into wall vases has already been mentioned, and they can also be inverted on a stand. You may be able to find someone to make you a wrought-iron stand, and if you are going to make a lot of use of such a container have two stands made – a low one for table centres and a taller stand for facing arrangements, both symmetrical and asymmetrical. Vegetable dishes and pans are often used to hold flowers – brass and copper frying pans are particularly effective when arranging red and orange flowers. The stand of a fondue pot makes an interesting container and even a cup and saucer can be used. With a little imagination a wealth of containers will be found in any kitchen.

A writing box can be successfully converted for use as a flower container. The arrangement here is an L-shaped one, using flowers in tints and shades of yellow. Part of the lid needs to be seen. The arrangement is described in detail in this chapter.

6 Accessories Used in Flower Arrangements

Blocks of glass Placed at the base of the flowers in a container in a line arrangement, they help to cover the pinholder and add an interesting addition to the arrangement. Position them so that they run through beneath the flowers and foliage. Colourless glass will resemble ice and give an illusion of coolness and so it is particularly lovely in summer arrangements. Coloured glass, though not as natural looking, can be useful to match a particular colour of flower. Some flowers never look happy with glass and chrysanthemums are one of these. Sometimes chunks of glass are impossible to obtain so, as an alternative, make your own by using glass from shattered car wind-

screens, which you can probably obtain from your local garage. Cover a pebble with silver paper, paste this over with a strong clear glue and then completely cover the pebble with two layers of the small pieces of glass. Shattered glass could also be used on its own. Blocks of glass can also look attractive when using only green flowers and leaves.

Pebbles These are used in a similar way to glass, but where certain flowers, such as chrysanthemums, do not look at home with glass, they will with the more ordinary-looking pebble, using a pebble with colouring to echo that of the flower. I have collected many different beautifully coloured pebbles from river banks and the

Below: A glass cake plate with a small glass dish containing florists' foam in the centre and five blocks of glass placed around the edge. Flowers are arranged in the florists' foam and merge with the blocks of glass.

Right: The glass cake plate arranged with paper-white narcissi and variegated scindapsus leaves. The arrangement is an all-round one and the blocks of glass merge with the flowers and leaves. Using the blocks of glass you do not need quite as much plant material. The scindapsus leaves go through with the flowers and also cover the florists' foam.

seashore – white, pink, grey, brown, mauve and some with metallic streaks. Pebbles need a container of heavy pottery or basketwork rather than porcelain and glass. Country-type arrangements using daffodils are good with pebbles.

If pebbles are placed beneath the water in a line arrangement in a dish, the colours of the pebbles are brighter. Both pebbles and glass should be placed so that a casual appearance is presented, but to achieve this, careful positioning is required so that they enhance the design of an arrangement and do not spoil the effect.

Shells and coral Many a happy moment can be spent on the seashore hunting for attractive shells which can be used in arrangements of seashore flowers such as the sea holly (*Eryngium*) or flowers, foliage and driftwood which remind us of the sea. A collection of different coloured ones for use with various coloured arrangements are useful.

A shell can also be used on its own as a container if it is large enough – this is mentioned in Chapter 5. Coral is very attractive as an accessory in an arrange-

ment, and can look splendid with many flowers.

Candles These make effective and useful accessories, especially when creating an arrangement in a candle cup. They are also attractive in the centre of long and low arrangements where they can give height. At Christmas and party time, incorporating candles immediately gives a festive air. A candle holder is placed in the centre of an arrangement or it can be positioned wherever the candle or candles are to be placed in the arrangement. Every care should be taken so that the candle is not likely to set fire to any of the plant material. A non-drip candle is preferable; make sure that the candle does not burn too low to the flowers. Match the candle to the colour of the flowers.

Fir cones A natural-looking accessory, which can be used in less sophisticated arrangements. Different shaped cones can be used, the more rounded or the longer and thinner type, depending on the plant material being used and the shape and style of the arrangement. Large cones can be used separately or

Useful accessories for the flower arranger. A piece of driftwood, pebbles, shells and coral can all be used on different occasions to add variety to an arrangement.

smaller ones can be 'sprayed up'. To do this, attach each cone to a wire by twisting a stub wire around the base of the cone so it is not noticeable, cover the wire with gutta percha, a florist's tape, and attach three or five cones by their wire stems to one long stub wire. This then makes them a spray. On festive occasions, cones can be sprayed with paint to match flowers or can be sprayed gold or silver or indeed any colour. A light spray is often more effective than spraying them completely. If you do not have access to woods to collect cones for yourself, they can usually be obtained fairly easily from shops.

Driftwood This is very much sought after by the flower arranger but it can be very difficult to find a piece with a really good shape. Although driftwood can be bought, it has often been bleached and is not always suitable for certain arrangements. It is usually preferable to use driftwood in its natural state, and you will certainly value it more if you are lucky enough to find a piece for yourself. Beaches and shores of lakes are the more likely hunting grounds. If it is the right shape, driftwood can form part of the actual container for the flowers, but generally it is used as an accessory and is particularly effective in simple arrange-

ments using only one variety of flower.

In this picture, the piece of driftwood – which I found by a lake – enables one to place a container into it. A small tin with a pinholder in it is placed on the wood, as can be seen, and held in place with Bostik Blu-tack. The flowers in the container are seven purple statice. This is a flower which dries well, but it is used here in its fresh state. The statice had several secondary stems and some of these are used lower in the container. Five mauvy-blue iris and the mauvy-coloured foliage of zebrina are also used.

Taking into consideration the shape of the driftwood, place a tall statice by the tallest part of the driftwood to follow this line higher. Another piece of statice goes on either side of it, each of the three pieces close together on the pinholder and each a different stem length. On the left side place another piece of statice, and low on the container on the right side a slightly shorter piece of statice. Next place in the five iris, a fairly small flower to the left of the centre at the top, the second flower a head shorter and going slightly to the right, the third flower again a head shorter going to the left edge, and the fourth and largest flower is shorter where the container meets the wood. Each of these iris go progressively forward on the pinholder. The fifth iris which is in the bud stage is placed horizontally on the left side. More statice is placed through with the flowers and also connects up the outline. The zebrina is also placed through with the flowers, some pieces curving over the edge at the base to make the flowers and driftwood look like one unit. Take care not to lose the shape of the driftwood. Check that the pinholder is covered.

Figurines For flower arrangements these are one or more objects which are on a single base. They are mainly used as an accessory in competitive flower arrangements, helping to interpret a theme like a song or book title, but should not be so noticeable as to detract from the flower arrangement. Often it would be very difficult to convey a particular theme in an arrangement if some additional figure was not used as well.

Drapes These are various coloured and textured materials to hang behind an arrangement to display the flowers to better effect, and are frequently used for exhibiting or in competitions. The drape can echo the colour of the arrangement or be contrasting – either way it can make an arrangement look more dramatic. Braid can be attached around the edge to make them look more attractive and better finished. They can be various sizes, depending on the size of the arrangement; a metre square is an average size. The materials can vary from silks and velvets for more sophisticated flowers and containers to the hessian material for country-type arrangements. At flower arrangement demonstrations, the demonstrator usually has a drape, sometimes attached to a wooden frame for easier handling, to hold up behind a completed arrangement.

The flowers arranged in the container on the driftwood are purple statice and mauvy iris with zebrina foliage. They are positioned as for a line arrangement, taking care not to hide the shape of the driftwood. A description of the arrangement is given in this chapter.

7 Methods of Holding Flowers in a Container

Putting wire netting into a container. In this instance the container is round with a pinholder in the centre. First roll the netting diagonally from one corner to the other, thus making four or five layers of netting. Secondly shape the netting to the container. Thirdly place it in the container and secure by clipping small pieces of netting over the edge. The method is described in detail in this chapter.

There are various methods used to hold plant material in a container, the main ones being wire netting, florists' foam and pinholders. The different ways these can be used are described in detail below. New products for securing flowers in arrangements often come on the market, and after each is tried and tested they usually have a particular part to play in flower arranging, but you will find your own favourite aid and probably use it most of the time. I must admit I still prefer, in the majority of arrangements, to use wire netting.

Wire netting

This is possibly the least costly way of holding flowers in a container. The netting is a wire mesh and I prefer the 50-mm (2-inch) size, as explained in Chapter 4. The pictures here demonstrate the correct way to place the netting in a container. First, select the size of the netting required, by considering the depth and width of the container. It is impossible to give exact measurements of a piece of netting needed for a certain container, as some people like a little more and others less. As a rough guide, however, a medium-sized bowl needs a 50-mm (2-inch) mesh about 450 to 700 mm (18 to 27 inches) wide and 450 mm (18 inches) high. It is much better to have one large piece of netting. If only two smaller pieces are available then it is advisable to join them together by twisting the edge of one around the other.

Next, loosely roll the netting from one corner to the other, so that you end up with four or five layers. After it has been rolled in this way consider the shape of the container to be used. With a bowl or tazza, the two ends need to be bent right into the centre and the netting gently forced into a rounded shape. With an urn, keep the netting narrow at the bottom then push it into the container. When a trough is being used, bend the ends of the netting in a little way on each side. Some of the netting should touch the bottom of the container and it should be level with the rim, and slightly raised in the centre where the longer stems are placed. Spread the netting evenly out in the container.

The next step is to secure the netting which can be done in two ways. If the container has a lip, some of the edges of the netting can be clipped over this. Five or six strands fastened at equal distances are sufficient to hold the netting firmly, and they will be hidden once the arrangement is completed. If there is no suitable lip then the netting will have to be tied into the container. Thirty-gauge silver reel wire is best for this purpose. If the silver wire is not available then a fairly fine string can be substituted. Tie the

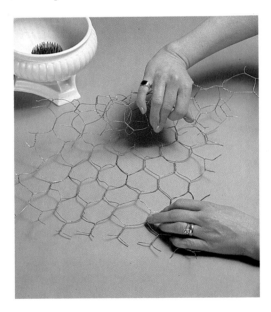

wire or string around the container as if you were tying up a parcel and finish by knotting firmly at the top of the netting. If the container has a stem then take the wire around this once or twice and then tie it both ways over the bowl. If, after the arrangement is completed, the wire or string is noticeable, it can be cut away and the flowers should remain in position. If you are using a china container then the netting could be secured with transparent sticky tape. However, never do this with valuable containers as it can mark them. This is especially true of silver, copper, brass, pewter and other metalware.

It is not necessary to remove the netting each time an arrangement is dismantled. Rinse the container thoroughly under the tap before putting it away and occasionally take out the netting and give

the vase a good scrub. It is a good idea to do this at the times of the year when the size of the stems get thicker or thinner; then one can put less netting or more netting as required when replacing it into the container.

When using wire netting in a fairly shallow container, a pinholder or a small piece of florists' foam can be placed at the bottom of the bowl, before the wire netting is placed into the container. This does help to anchor the longer-stemmed flowers and make a firmer start to the arrangement.

Florists' foam

In Chapter 4 I explained what florists' foam was and that it needs to be soaked. It should be soaked for at least two hours and preferably overnight. Keep florists'

This red asymmetrical arrangement in a brown ovenware dish is arranged in wire netting with a pinholder under it in one corner to hold the tallest flowers. It is completed as for a basic asymmetrical arrangement and the flowers are five stems of red spray carnations, three red cyclamen and three red roses, with cotoneaster berries and foliage of Mahonia aquifolia *and small ferns.*

Below: Dampened florists' foam placed in a polythene bag with wire netting over it can be used as a base in which to position flowers for a pew end or to go on a pillar or pole. The length of the wire coat hanger which is used for hooking the arrangement into position will vary according to where it is to be placed.

foam under water initially and help it to absorb water more quickly by weighting it down. Never arrange the flowers in dry florists' foam and then fill the container with water.

The use of florists' foam is an exceptionally good method of holding flowers in a container when transporting it to another place, either for giving as a gift or for competitive display. You will then be sure that the water will not spill, but when at your destination make sure that a little water is poured into the container, so that the florists' foam is kept moist at all times. If it is being given as a present then a label, saying 'please keep wet', is a good idea.

When using a small container with florists' foam, make sure that a small space is left so that one is able to pour in water. The florists' foam needs either to be wedged into position or sticky tape needs to be placed across the top of the vase to hold it in place. Do not use the sticky tape method if the vase is valuable as it may mark it. One can also use florists' foam on its own in large containers but the disadvantages are that it can be rather costly and also one can only obtain a block roughly the size of a brick, and this is not always large enough. Using two pieces in a container is not very satisfactory, so it is better to use a large block of florists' foam with wire netting over it. It is easier to use florists' foam with hard-stemmed flowers rather than soft-stemmed, as these tend to break when they are pushed into the foam. The best way to place soft stems into foam is to make a hole in it first with a piece of stick.

Florists' foam can be used in any shape of vase, urn, trough, tazza, bowl, etc. but remember to leave a small space to pour water into when topping up the container, as the foam can dry out quite quickly.

Line arrangements on flat plates and dishes can have a piece of florists' foam instead of a pinholder on which to arrange the plant material. The foam can be anchored onto a florists' foam holder, as explained in Chapter 4. If the flowers being used are not too heavy the foam can be used on its own, preferably placed in a small container on the plate, so as not to have water on the plate. The foam could also have a piece of netting over the top for this type of arrangement.

Florists' foam is very useful when arranging a spray of flowers for a pew end or for hanging onto a pillar in church. To do this one needs to soak the foam and place it in a polythene bag, place wire netting around this and make a hook at the back with stub wires or with a wire coat hanger, to enable it to be hung up

more easily. The flowers and foliage are then arranged directly into the florists' foam by piercing the stems through the polythene; occasionally if the stems are not very stiff you may need to make a hole first with a woody stem. You will find when the foam is first pierced the water will drip through for a while but this eventually stops. Make sure the florists' foam is kept damp but do not put too much water in the polythene bag. Also spray the flowers overhead with a mist sprayer to make sure the flowers keep really fresh.

Cradles can be made for florists' foam, which are used when an arrangement is being placed in a glass or crystal vase. Although it is quite in order to see clean flower stems through the glass, you do not really want to see wire netting or foam as this can look ugly. Take a small piece of wire netting and push the centre about 50 mm (2 inches) down inside the container and clip the edges around the rim. When this netting is firmly in position, put in the soaked foam so that it comes just above the rim of the glass container, as shown in the picture. Three-quarters fill the vase with water. The stems of the tallest flowers at the back can go straight down into the container. Other stems of flowers and foliage only go into the foam; the flowers which come out over the edge of the container should be placed into the foam horizontally. Make sure that the leaves and flowers over the edge cover the foam cradle, as it should not be seen in the completed arrangement.

The flowers in shades of yellow have been arranged in florists' foam in a small and shallow container made of wrought iron set on a stem also of wrought-iron. Foam has been used as wire netting would not hold the flowers sufficiently in a shallow container. The foam is a little higher than the rim of the container with wire netting over it. In turn, reel wire has been tied over the netting and the wire has been twisted round the base of the small container to hold it securely into position. Again, do not fill the container completely with florists' foam but leave a space in which water can be poured.

The arrangement is a basic facing arrangement and the flowers used are three stems of alstroemeria (Peruvian lily), 11 stems of winter jasmine, nine freesia, two stems of spray chrysanthemums, five roses, three yellow arum lilies and erica. The foliage is hebe, vinca (periwinkle), euonymus and scindapsus. The secondary stems of the alstroemeria and spray chrysanthemum were taken from the main stem and used individually, as it is a relatively small arrangement.

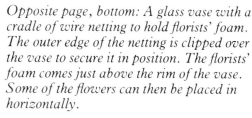

As the stems are all quite hard with the exception of the arums, they were fairly easy to place into the florists' foam. A small hole was made with a stick when placing in the arums.

The main outline flowers are placed in first, the tallest flower at the top being a jasmine which is placed three-quarters of the way back in the container in the centre. A freesia is placed next, on the right of the jasmine and is a little shorter, another jasmine is placed on the left of the centre flower a little shorter still, making three differing lengths at the top of the arrangement. The widest points go in next and are low on the container and three-quarters of the way back. On the right goes a jasmine and on the left a freesia, both being the same length over the edge of the vase; the height is roughly

the overall width. A freesia is the longest flower at the front and is in a line with the tallest flower at the back.

Place the main flowers, the arums, and the three leaves of scindapsus in the centre of the arrangement. One arum is placed fairly high at the back, one to the right of the longest flower at the front, and the third and largest flower low to the left of the centre. Framing these three arums are the three scindapsus leaves.

Next go to the outline and graduate the length of stems quite sharply, to achieve a triangular rather than a fan shape. The grouping of this arrangement is jasmine, alstroemeria, hebe and vinca going high on the left to low on the right, and freesia, roses, spray chrysanthemum, euonymus and erica going in the opposite direction; the roses are kept fairly near the centre.

When the flowers and foliage have been placed on the periphery, place some foliage through the arrangement, putting in some short pieces to cover the florists' foam and wire netting. Place other flowers throughout the arrangement, with some coming low to cover the edge of the container. These are placed low in the florists' foam, but still using the natural curves of the stems. The stems should all radiate from the centre, as explained in Chapter 2, and there should be plenty of variation of stem length. Check that the mechanics of the arrangement are covered.

Pinholders

These are used in various kinds of flower arrangements. When used on a flat dish or plate for a line arrangement, it needs to be a heavy-based one. Place it on the plate in the position the tallest flower is going to be. If a less heavy pinholder is used, then it is an advantage to attach it to the container with plasticine or a re-usable adhesive such as Bostik Blu-tack. If a flat dish is being used, place the pinholder in a small container, just large enough to hold the pinholder, into which the water is poured. A painted salmon tin could be used for this. When arranging flowers on a pinholder, place the tallest flowers first before positioning the horizontal flowers to establish the width. This helps to balance the flowers and will stop them from toppling over.

Pinholders can be used under wire netting in containers. They are placed in the position in which the tallest flowers at the back are to be placed. This can save much impatience as it will prevent the longer-stemmed flowers moving. In an all-round arrangement a pinholder is placed in the centre of the container as the longer flowers go in there. It is also placed in the centre of a trough for a table centre.

It is unnecessary to use a pinholder under wire netting in deep containers such as urns, cylinders, etc. as the flowers have such a long way to go into the netting that they are held firmly into position.

Cones and tubes

These are sometimes used to hold flowers when doing large pedestal arrangements if longer-stemmed flowers are required than the flowers which are available. The cones are placed into the arrangement and if necessary attached to a stick as explained in Chapter 4. Wire netting or florists' foam is placed into them and flowers are placed into the cone. They can also be used to place fresh flowers into a dried arrangement to add interest to it, or to add fresh flowers when doing a planted garden with pot plants.

An arrangement on a board which has a mat stuck to it. A small metal dish containing a pinholder is placed towards the side of the board, with a piece of driftwood in front of it. On the dish are three fir branches, Muscari *and* Helleborus foetidus.

8 What to Grow

All flower arrangers have their favourite plant materials, and although one can do lovely arrangements by buying from the florist and also picking from the hedgerow, it is pleasant to feel that you can go into the garden and select the special pieces you are particularly fond of, such as a particular colour or shape of flower or foliage, to enhance your arrangements.

I find it more helpful to grow special foliages rather than flowers, as flowers in superb condition are generally easily obtainable in the local florist, whereas interesting foliage may be more difficult to buy. One can grow such a wide selection of different coloured leaves: limy-green, grey-green, blue-green, red, apricot, orange, yellow. Of course some of these colours are only available at certain times of the year, but as the seasons come round you can take advantage of the different colourings to vary your arrangements.

I am now going to mention various foliages which I find are helpful in flower arranging; some, of course, will not grow in all soils but I am sure that there are some which would grow well in your garden. There are many varieties of *Hedera* (ivies) which are so hardy they can be in constant use; the larger varieties include *Hedera canariensis*, and *Hedera colchica dentata aurea*, which is a variegated golden colour, climbs up walls and is striking for use with yellow flowers. It can be used in sprays in large pedestal arrangements or as single leaves, especially as the main leaf in the centre in smaller arrangements. Sprays of small-leafed ivies, such as *Hedera helix* 'Jubilee', can be used in smaller arrangements. Many ivies come in grey-green colourings, some variegated and some tinged with pink, especially in the winter. The grey and pink colouring blends well with pink flowers.

The mahonias are good for fairly large arrangements, especially *Mahonia bealei*; this has an attractive red tinge in winter and consequently goes well with red flowers, particularly chrysanthemums. The smaller-leaved *Mahonia aquifolia* is also a good standby – when other foliage may be damaged by the weather, it is usually in a fairly good condition to use. Both varieties are quite hardy.

Elaeagnus pungens 'Maculata' is a variegated-leafed shrub which is deep golden with a green edge. Being a hardy shrub it is very useful for foliage in the winter. It is marvellous in yellow arrangements, and when doing mixed foliage arrangements it is good for the variety of colours. The backs of the leaves are silvery so if the leaves are placed downwards this gives more interest to a foliage arrangement.

The clean-cut looking leaves of the *Skimmia japonica* can be used all the year round as it is an evergreen shrub. It has an added bonus of having large clusters of red berries through the winter.

The golden privet, *Ligustrum ovalifolium* 'Variegatum' is attractive for its

Hedera colchica dentata aurea is a variegated ivy which can be used singly or in sprays and looks attractive with yellow flowers.

green and yellow leaves which, being quite small, are useful in smaller arrangements as well as larger ones.

Hebes are used mainly for their foliage rather than for their flowers. There are a great many varieties in many shades of green and also variegated ones. You can choose from grey-green, yellow-green, green, etc. The grey-green is good with blue and pink flowers and enhances an arrangement. The variegated variety is not as hardy as the plain green varieties. These are used in small arrangements as the leaves on the stems are dainty. Euonymus leaves can be used in a similar way to hebes.

Ruta graveolens, which is rue or the herb of grace, is attractive in flower arrangements for the shape of its leaf, as well as its bluey-grey colouring. It is a more 'fussy' leaf than many, so is most useful in smaller arrangements. Its yellow flowers are not used as much as its leaves. There is also a variegated variety which is quite unusual and not so readily obtainable but again is very useful to the flower arranger. Probably the best known of the blue-grey rues is *Ruta graveolens* 'Jackman's Blue'.

The grey foliage of *Senecio greyii* is useful for its colour and also because it is an evergreen and so available throughout

Top left: Euonymus japonica aurea *has an attractively coloured leaf which looks good in arrangements.*

Top right: Mahonia japonica *is useful in flower arranging all the year round.*

Above left: Mahonia aquifolia *is a good standby in the winter when there is a shortage of foliage.*

Above right: Hedera helix 'Jubilee' *has fairly small leaves and so it is useful for smaller arrangements.*

the year. The flowers are not particularly significant, but its leaves are grey-green at the front and silvery-grey at the back. Another grey foliage, but this time with more feathery leaves, is santolina, which makes an interesting shape for mixed foliage arrangements and also looks well with pink and blue flowers. It is an evergreen so is worth growing for this reason.

The flower arranger often needs large single leaves for the centre of an arrangement in colours to blend with a particular arrangement. The hosta (funkia or plantain lily) has a most attractive leaf to use in the summer – it always seems such a pity when the plant dies down in the autumn and I await with impatience for it to re-emerge again in the spring. As these are such beautiful leaves and come in various forms I will name some of the varieties which are among my favourites. *Hosta crispula* is green with a broad white margin; *Hosta fortunei* – limy-green with darker edges. *Hosta plantaginea grandiflora* is plain green and although it is not as attractive as some varieties it does have very large leaves and so is very helpful in large pedestal arrangements. *Hosta sieboldiana* is another large variety but its leaves are blue-green in colour with a ribbed effect. *Hosta undulata* is a variegated variety. So, as you can appreciate, with the various shades of green and some being variegated, they are indeed useful. The flowers can also be attractive as they are fairly tall and spiky in shades of mauve and also some varieties in white. They can look very elegant in an urn with just their own leaves or as a simple arrangement on a pinholder.

Another splendid large leaf, which this time is available all year round, is the green roundish leaf of the bergenia or, as some people call it, elephant's ear. In winter it is often tinged with red or orange, and so is useful to use with red or orange flowers at this time of year. The leaves vary in size but are generally large,

Opposite page, top left: Senecio laxifolium *has grey-coloured foliage and is especially good with pink and blue flowers.*

Opposite page, top right: Hosta crispula *is often used as the large leaf in the centre of arrangements, particularly with white flowers.*

Opposite page, bottom left: Another useful variety of hosta, the Hosta fortunei 'Albo picta'.

Opposite page, bottom right: Berberis stenophylla *has lovely arched sprays.*

Below: Berberis thunbergii, *like other varieties of this plant, is worth using even though it is very prickly.*

Below right: Cotoneaster horizonitalis *has many berries in the autumn.*

though some are small enough for the centre of a medium-sized arrangement. In spring it has pretty pink flowers which are small with many clustered on a stem, and these can make quite pleasing arrangements. There are different varieties of bergenia and some leaves tend to be more oval than others; these are not as hardy.

Artichoke leaves are good for large groups. The grey, irregular, pointed leaves are an attractive shape for the centre of an arrangement, and go well with white, pink, blue and also red flowers. Of course you can always use the flower for arranging as well.

For smaller arrangements, particularly line arrangements, the *Arum italicum* 'Pictum' with its splendid marbled-effect leaves is a good choice. The large arum (*Zantedeschia*) leaves are also good, especially when using the flower as well. The cornus or dogwood is mainly used for its red stems in winter, but it has an attractive foliage at other times of the year.

Berries are essential for autumn arrangements. There are so many kinds and many different coloured ones that you can usually find varieties to suit the soil in your garden. The berberis family has many beautiful coloured berries; the bluish mauve of *Berberis darwinii*, which come in the summer, the coral colour of *Berberis wilsonae*, the red berries of *Berberis thunbergii* 'Atropurpurea' which has brilliant scarlet foliage in the autumn. These are all worth growing in the garden for flower arrangement, even if they are slightly prickly to arrange! Cotoneasters also have many different coloured berries, the *Cotoneaster horizontalis* being a

well-known variety with its many scarlet berries in the autumn. *Cotoneaster franchetii* has orangy berries which are also attractive to use in their green stage, in fact in all their changing colours. *Cotoneaster* 'Exburiensis' has large bunches of yellow berries.

The *Leycesteria formosa* (Himalayan honeysuckle) has lovely hanging sprays of aubergine-coloured berries, and is attractive to use with aubergine in a fruit group. To show the berries to their best advantage remove some of the large leaves from around the berries. The flowers of the leycesteria which are very dark red are also quite impressive in an arrangement. *Symphoricarpus albus* 'Laevigatus' (snowberry) has white berries which often stay on the shrub through the winter, and you can also get pink-berried varieties. The snowberry has lovely arching sprays, suitable for use in both small and fairly large arrangements. A shrub which has quite unusual berries is pernettya, unusual in that pink and white ones grow together on the same shrub.

As well as sprays of berries to use in arrangements, it is rewarding to grow flowering shrubs. These are helpful in many arrangements, especially the line arrangements. The viburnum family has a variety of flowering shrubs but the prettiest one is the *Viburnum fragans*, with its sweet-smelling, pale pink flowers. *Viburnum opulus* 'Sterile' is useful for its round ball-like flowers, which for arranging purposes are best used in their green stage, before they go white. But do not be tempted to cut them before the green flowers are open because they tend not to keep well in water if picked too early.

As well as being lovely for their scent indoors, the daphnes are delightful in small arrangements; with flowers coloured creamy, pink and mauve they are all most attractive. My favourite colour is the *Daphne odora* 'Aureomarginata' which has variegated foliage. Spiraea with its small leaves and delicate white flowers produced on arching sprays is perfect for a free-flowing arrangement. Broom (*Cytisus*) is a good shrub to grow, not only for the wealth of different coloured flowers such as creams, yellows, pinks, reds, bronze, etc. but also for the spiky form of its branches, which adds much interest to arrangements rather than having all leaves which are round or oval.

There are several varieties of jasmines. *Jasminum nudiflorum* is the winter-flowering one, with dainty yellow flowers yet hardy enough to withstand very cold weather. The summer-flowering one, *Jasminum officinale*, is very sweet-smelling and has lovely sprays of white flowers.

In spring the flowering cherries, of which there are many varieties, are very useful; their lovely branches can be placed on a pinholder on their own with just a few large leaves around the base. Two good varieties to grow are *Prunus cerasifera* 'Atropurpurea' with its red coloured foliage and the double pink *Prunus triloba*.

Interesting plants with twisted shapes are the corkscrew hazel (*Corylus avellana* 'Contorta'), which has catkins in the spring, and the willow, *Salix matsudana* 'Tortuosa'. Both these plants are exceptionally good for line arrangements, as their branch shapes are so intriguing; too mixed an arrangement would detract from

their fascinating shapes. The witch hazel (*Hamamelis mollis*) is superb in the winter; with its clusters of yellow and brown flowers on bare branches, it is again ideal for the simpler arrangements. Another winter-flowering shrub which looks best arranged simply is the *Chimonauthus praecox* (winter sweet) which has delicate creamy flowers on its bare branches.

The best flowers to grow in the garden for flower arrangement are the slightly more unusual ones, those with colours that are going to be particularly helpful or those you might have difficulty in obtaining from the florists. Two flowers suitable for small arrangements and a little more unusual than the ordinary flowers are *Fritallaria meleagris* (snakes head fritillary), which is purple and white – one variety is white with a greenish tinge – and *Anemone blanda*, the mountain wind flower of Greece which flowers in the late winter.

The hellebores are super to have as they also flower in winter time. *Helleborus niger* (Christmas rose) is white, *Helleborus orientalis* (Lenten rose) is mauvy-green, though some are pale pink, and *Helleborus foetidus* is not chosen for its pleasant smell but for its lovely green colour, the flowers being small and in bunches.

I like to grow green flowers because I think limy-green colours do sharpen an arrangement, especially if using mixed flowers, and also the shapes of the flowers are good when doing a mixed green arrangement. *Mollucella laevis* (bells of Ireland) has small bell-like flowers right up its long pointed stem; as it dries well it can be used in dried arrangements too.

Above left: Many varieties of viburnum can be grown to use for flower arranging.

Above: The yellow flowers of Jasminum nudiflorum *are a welcome sight in the winter.*

Opposite page, top: This arrangement uses plant material cut from the garden. The flowers and foliage are arranged in an oblong tin placed at the base of the brass tray. The plant material, consisting of broom, golden privet, hebe, three bergenia leaves and winter jasmine flowers, is arranged around part of the tray, with the broom and privet curving naturally over it.

Opposite page, bottom left: Flowering prunus is useful for large groups of flowers.

Opposite page, bottom right: Helleborus niger (Christmas rose) *flowers in the winter and is used in small arrangements.*

The *Euphorbia wulfenii* is bluish-green and has greenish-yellow bracts. Other very useful euphorbia are *E. griffithii* which is bright yellow and *E. polychroma* which is gold. For summer the green nicotiana (tobacco plant) is good as is the very popular *Alchemilla mollis* (lady's mantle); this is probably the most used of the green flowers by flower arrangers as it is easy to grow, and in no time at all you can have small plants growing all over the garden.

Ericas (heathers) can be used all year round, and if several different varieties are grown in the garden one is usually flowering, either pink, white, mauve or dark red. When they are not flowering they can be used for their attractive coloured foliage.

Crocosmia, the large montbretia, is such a bright orange that I like to include this in the garden. The *Iris foetidissima* is excellent to grow for its fine orange seedhead. I also like to grow flag iris for the usefulness of the spiky leaves rather than the flowers.

Polygonatum multiflorum (Solomon's seal) grows well and the curved stem with small white flowers along it makes a very good shape for flower arrangements. Another white flower I particularly like is the philadelphus (mock orange blossom); if the leaves are too overpowering a few can be carefully removed near the flowers.

There are various types of arrangements that could be achieved using flowers from the garden. Perhaps one of the nicest ways with a country-type arrangement is in a basket with mixed flowers – just a few of each kind of flower in mixed colours, preferably excluding white but including lime-green and yellow. The arrangement in the all-round basket, which has metal lining in which a pinholder and wire netting has been placed, includes summer flowers: yellow iris, blue delphinium, red antirrhinums mauve statice, purple flag iris, orange marigolds, mauve sweet peas, pink and red stock, red rhododendron, red sweet williams, green alchemilla and orange and yellow roses. The foliage is in grey, *Lamium* and *Stachys lanata*. Commence the arrangement in the same way as the basic all-round with mixed coloured flowers in Chapter 11, page 80. Keep the flowers going from side to side so colours and shapes are on both sides. Have nine outline points around the edge for this size basket. Make sure the handle is visible. Have a light-coloured flower for the top, in this case a yellow iris. Group the foliage – not too much is needed for this arrangement.

The following facing arrangement in the basket with a handle incorporates spring flowers. Again the basket has a lining with a pinholder and netting in it. The flowers and foliage are two different kinds of daffodils and the narcissus Soleil d'Or, yellow tulips, tree ivy and trailing ivy and five bergenia leaves. The branches are forsythia and hazel catkins. The arrangement is as for a basic facing arrangement, but as the basket has a handle this must be kept fairly free. Choose to group the flowers so that the arrangement will look balanced in both the amount of material each way and also in the shapes chosen for each group.

The arrangement in the brass bowl uses autumn flowers, and to match the brass the flowers from the garden are in yellow and green and include dahlias,

Below: There are many varieties of ericas (heathers) and many colours. It is an advantage to have a good selection so that there is at least one flowering at any time of the year. Ericas are also useful on account of the colouring of their foliage.

Below right: Philadelphus is equally suitable for large or small arrangements as whole branches of it can be used or just the small side pieces from the stem.

Above: A facing arrangement in a brown ovenware dish with garden plants. These are arranged in clumps as if they were growing, with bun moss covering the wire netting between the flowers. In the centre are some stems of dogwood (Cornus alba). *Cotoneaster and skimmia clumps are placed high on the right to low on the left, heather and* Helleborus foetidus *are grouped the opposite way, and a bunch of primroses is positioned in the centre.*

Left: An all-round arrangement in a wicker basket with a handle. The flowers, which are different colours and shapes, are cut from the garden, only two or three of each variety being used. A description of the arrangement is given in this chapter.

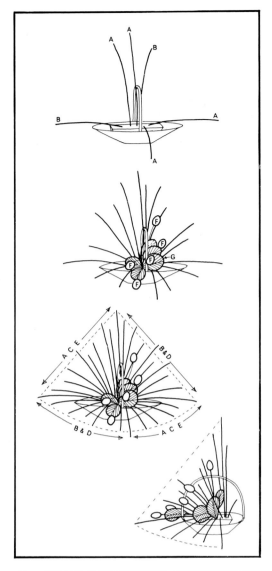

Above left: Line drawings to show a facing arrangement in a basket. The first diagram has the six outline points, while in the second flowers have been added on the outline and the centre flowers and leaves are placed in position. The third diagram shows the overall shape and the fourth a side view of how the arrangement should be built out from the tallest flower to the longest ones over the front edge. The flowers and foliage used are forsythia (A), catkins (B), Fortune narcissi (C), daffodils (D), Soleil d'Or narcissi (E), tulips (F) and bergenia leaves (G).

Above: The completed arrangement of mixed spring flowers, which are particularly suited to a wicker basket. Tree ivy and trailing ivy fills the spaces between the flowers but part of the basket handle should remain visible. Details of the arrangement are given in this chapter.

Left: Yellow garden flowers as an all-round arrangement in a brass bowl. The arrangement is lower than a basic all-round one so it would be suitable for the centre of a table.

Right: A table centre of mixed shades of roses from the garden accompanied by their own foliage.

Below: This facing arrangement of lilies of the valley in a cupid container is kept low and wide, taking into account the shape of the shell on top of the figure. Ivy is placed in with the flowers.

chrysanthemums and green nicotiana, seedheads of hypericum and golden rod. The all-round arrangement is lower than a basic all-round so that it can be used as a table centre. The foliage also matches the colouring of the flowers and is skimmia, golden privet, variegated rue, bergenia leaves and philadelphus foliage.

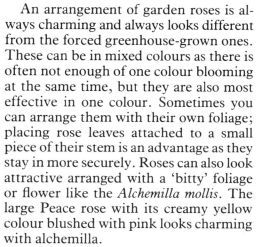

An arrangement of garden roses is always charming and always looks different from the forced greenhouse-grown ones. These can be in mixed colours as there is often not enough of one colour blooming at the same time, but they are also most effective in one colour. Sometimes you can arrange them with their own foliage; placing rose leaves attached to a small piece of their stem is an advantage as they stay in more securely. Roses can also look attractive arranged with a 'bitty' foliage or flower like the *Alchemilla mollis*. The large Peace rose with its creamy yellow colour blushed with pink looks charming with alchemilla.

Often there is a mass of lily of the valley in the garden and you can gather a large bunch. These have much firmer stems than the forced greenhouse-grown ones, so this is where you can have a dainty arrangement with the added advantage of a lovely perfume, such as the one in the small cupid container of white china. It is arranged as a facing arrangement but is kept lower and wider in keeping with the shape of the shell on the top of the figure. Florists' foam can be used in a small container like this and a piece of netting can also be placed over it. Some of the leaves of the lily of the valley are used and also green trailing ivy leaves. Keep the flowers a little shorter over the container at the front so that the face of the cupid can be seen.

In winter you can go out into the garden and cut just a few twigs and a few leaves at the base of the branches of the

Above: Cyclamen persicum. *The leaves of cyclamen can be used with their own flowers or in a mixed-flower arrangement. The cut flowers can be used on their own or with mixed flowers in shades of one colour.*

hardier plants like bergenia. These can be arranged in various containers such as the heavier kind of pottery or as a line arrangement using a pinholder. A garden on a meat plate or some other dish or basket is very quick to arrange. You can cut a lovely selection of flowers from the garden but it does need to be damp enough to grow the bun moss to place over the container.

If you are fortunate enough to have a garden the ideas for arrangements are literally endless. However, I do not want those without a garden to think I have forgotten them, as it is possible to grow quite a lot on a balcony or in a window-box or as pot plants indoors for flower arranging. A few pot plants are useful for any flower arranger, especially in the winter. Many ivies grow well both indoors and on balconies. Hebes and heathers can be planted on balconies, and if you grow herbs for your cooking these could be used in flower arrangements too. Sage is good and some varieties come in a grey-mauve colouring – there is also a variegated one. Rue is also an attractive herb.

The sedum pot plant grows well and pieces can be cut from it. Geraniums have very attractive leaves for a flower arrangement as they come in many colours. The flowers are also good in arrangements as the colours are so lovely and bright. Cyclamen flowers too could be taken from a pot plant. Make sure you condition them as described in Chapter 9, as for Christmas roses (*Helleborus niger*), before arranging them in a container.

Scindapsus are excellent to take from the plant as they are fairly large leaves and also keep well in water. They are good used as the centre leaves in a medium or small arrangement. Caladiums can be used as a whole plant as a focal point in a pedestal arrangement. *Begonia rex* is another leaf which is suitable for the centre of an arrangement because of its lovely coloured leaves. I hope after this there will be some leaves and flowers left on your pot plants!

Above left: Sedum sieboldii '*Medio-variegata*'. *Sedum are useful pot plants to grow for flower arranging. The pretty foliage can be used in small arrangements and keeps well when cut.*

Above: Pelargonium '*Mrs Quilter*'. *Many varieties of geranium are attractive in flower arrangements. The brightly coloured flowers are good for Victorian-type arrangements and the leaves can also be used.*

9 How to Condition Flowers and Foliage

When flowers and foliage are cut from the garden or from a pot plant, or brought home from the florists, before arranging them time needs to be spent giving the plant material the necessary treatment to make them last longer when they are arranged in the container. All flowers and foliage benefit from a long drink in a deep bucket which has been almost filled with tepid water. If the flowers have been bought from a flower shop the florist has probably had them in water for a time – but as you do not know how long, there is no harm in making sure by giving them a long drink.

Before placing the flowers in the bucket, the ends of the stems should be treated so that they will take up water more readily. This preparation is necessary because, after the flowers have been cut, the sap at the end of each stem dries quickly and forms a seal. The following treatments should be carried out, both when the flowers are given their initial drink, and also, if you need to recut them again, when they are finally arranged. Remember to put the flowers into water immediately after they have been prepared.

Soft stems e.g. tulip, arum lily. These can usually take up water easily. Cut each stem on the slant, never straight across as there is a danger that it will rest on the bottom of the bucket – or, if arranged, the container – and will be unable to take up sufficient water. This cannot happen when the stem is cut at an angle as it rests on the point. Such a cut will also give a larger area through which the stem can drink.

Hard and wood stems e.g. carnations and chrysanthemums. These have greater difficulty in absorbing water than soft-stemmed flowers and foliage. Make a slit up the centre of the end of each stem for about 25 mm (1 inch). Alternatively, hammer the end of each woody stem so that the tissues are crushed. Hammering woody stems can be quicker when preparing them for the initial drink, but when cutting them to the required length for an arrangement, it is more convenient to slit them.

Hollow stems e.g. lupins and delphiniums. When flowers with hollow stems are placed in water, their tip ends always turn upwards which tends to spoil the final arrangement. To prevent this, turn each flower upside down over the sink, and with a small watering-can fill the stem with water. Do this very carefully to avoid air bubbles forming. Then you can either plug the stem with a small piece of florists' foam or cotton wool and place it in the bucket of tepid water, or you can simply hold your thumb over the bottom of the stem, put it into the water and take your thumb away. The pressure of water in the bucket will keep the stem filled with water. When you cut the stem to the length that the arrangement

It is better to cut soft-stemmed flowers at an angle as shown on the tulip on the right, not straight across as on the left.

63

Below: Hard-stemmed flowers need to be cut up the centre of the stem from the bottom as shown with this carnation.

Above right: Another way of enabling a flower such as chrysanthemum, which has a hard or woody stem, to take up water more easily is to hammer the end of the stem.

Right: Treatment for a wilting rose is to place the bottom of the stem in 25 mm (1 inch) of boiling water, protecting the head with tissue paper.

requires, do this under the water. If you need to cut a treated stem when it is out of the water, turn it upside down. You can cut it to the required length without losing water.

Hot water treatment e.g. dahlias and young spring foliage. These plant materials will benefit from the hot water treatment as will flowers which droop after they have been in an arrangement for a day or two; this happens particularly to greenhouse-grown roses. To revive them dip the ends of the stems in boiling water. Bring a pan of water to the boil and place the bottom 25 mm (1 inch) of the stems in the water, having first protected the flower heads from the steam by wrapping them in either tissue paper or polythene bags. Leave them in the water for about 20 seconds and then take them out and place in tepid water which comes nearly up to their heads.

Burning stems e.g. euphorbias and poppies. When these flowers are cut they give off a white milky substance and they are said to be 'bleeding'. Holding the ends of such stems in a match or gas flame for a few seconds will stop the bleeding and they will be able to absorb water more easily. The petals should be protected while the stem is over the flame, preferably by placing the head of the flower in a polythene bag as this is safer than using tissue paper near a flame.

Cutting the side of a flower stem e.g. hellebores, cyclamen and polyanthus. These flowers will last very much longer if their stems are slit up about 25 mm (1 inch) on one side, starting 25 mm from the bottom.

Submerging certain flowers and foliage e.g. young spring foliage, artichoke leaves, violets and hydrangeas. These all benefit if they are completely submerged while being given their initial drink. Violets take in a great deal of water through their petals, and even after submerging them for the first drink, it is advantageous to spray them overhead occasionally in the arrangement. If hydrangeas wilt after they have been arranged, as they will sometimes if they are cut when they are not fully mature, they can be revived by placing the flower heads in water. They will take in water through their bracts and quickly be refreshed.

Above: The side of a stem of Helleborus niger *(Christmas rose) is slit with a knife about 25 mm (1 inch) up from the bottom of the stem for about 25 mm.*

Above: Submerging a leaf which is soft for its initial drink. This also helps flowers such as hydrangea.

Stripping the bark from the bottom of a stem of lilac for about 100 mm (4 inches) to enable it to take up water more easily. The bottom of the stem also needs to be split or hammered.

Removing bark from the bottom of a stem e.g. lilac and guelder rose. With flowers such as these, it is advisable to strip the bark from the bottom of the stem for about 100 mm (4 inches) as well as splitting the stems or hammering, as water is then absorbed more readily.

General hints on the care of flowers

It is preferable to use warm water for the first drink as flowers are refreshed more quickly than when cold water is used. When the flowers have their initial drink it is a good idea to leave them in a deep bucket overnight or for at least two to three hours. It is important that flowers are not left out of water for too long as they wilt very quickly. The anemone is particularly vulnerable. Sometimes it is necessary to keep flowers for a time before they are arranged. If this is the case, first treat them, put them in a bucket for their initial drink and then place this in a cool place, preferably on a stone floor. Roses can be rolled tightly in greaseproof paper to stop them opening too quickly.

Tulips, as everyone knows, are not easy flowers to arrange because their stems curve towards the light. The stems can be straightened by rolling them tightly in greaseproof paper and then placing them in deep water. Unfortunately, after a day in an arrangement, they will tend to revert to their old ways.

To encourage flowers to open more rapidly, place them in fairly warm water. With gladioli, if the flowers are not opening when required, remove the top two or three buds, so that the flowers lower down the stem will open more quickly, then place them in warm water. Roses can be gently blown into so that they will open slightly quicker.

Before flowers and foliage are arranged, the leaves which will be submerged should be removed. If these are left on, the water will quickly smell unpleasant, but with clean stems it should stay comparatively fresh. It is not usually necessary to change the water once the flowers have been arranged, but if clean water is needed, it should be tepid. The water level in the container holding the flowers should be looked at each day. On the first day it is advisable to look at it night and morning, as flowers take more water when they are first arranged, but afterwards once a day should be sufficient provided the room they are in is not excessively hot. When topping up, use tepid water as the water in the container can become fairly warm and it is rather a shock to the flowers if they are suddenly given cold water.

Some leaves and flowers have 'hairy' stems, for example, *Begonia rex*, which can act as a siphon draining water out of the container to leave a pool of water on the furniture. To avoid this, remove the

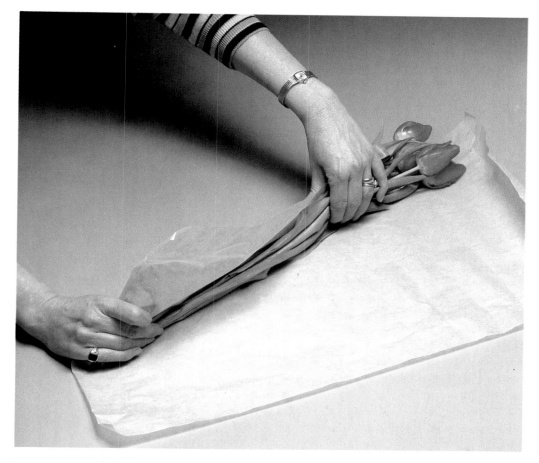

Placing a bunch of tulips on greaseproof paper prior to rolling them. Rolling tightly helps to keep the stems straight.

The bunch of tulips rolled in the greaseproof paper before being placed in a bucket of deep water.

hairs from that part of the stem which goes beneath the water by scraping it. Branches of lichen need to have the ends of their stems cleaned for the same reason.

When cutting a stem of foliage or a flowering branch from a tree it is best to cut it at a joint where the twig or branch meets a larger twig or branch. Cutting it here makes it less noticeable that a piece has been removed from the tree. It is preferable to cut it at the back of the twig or branch so one cannot see the scar. This also applies when side pieces of arranged flowers need to be removed.

10 Colour

Colour plays a large part in successful flower arranging. If an arrangement has good colour balance but is lacking in other respects it will still be attractive and receive attention. The appreciation of colour is a very personal thing and I am purposely not going to be over technical. Rather, I am going to give some suggestions for colour schemes which I hope will help you.

Monochromatic

This is a colour scheme which uses the tints and shades of one particular colour or hue. Some of the most successful flower arrangements are achieved by using this colour scheme which can be very attractive. A 'tint' is a hue with white added and a 'shade' is a hue with black added. It is worth taking extra care to make sure that the colours are correct. For example, with pink flowers you will need to use either the blue-pinks or the yellow-pinks as mixing the two will not give the blending of colours necessary for this scheme. You will soon acquire a flair for this, however, although it is not always easy to obtain just the colour of flower which one requires to do this kind of arrangement. It is impossible for a florist to carry a full range of all colours, and often you will not have the right selection in your garden.

Clashing colours

The scheme on page 71 uses the clashing colours contained in one hue and can be great fun. For a red arrangement you will need the blue-reds and also the yellow-reds, going from magenta to bright orange. This may sound dreadful but it is surprising how attractive it can look, especially on a dinner table or for a party, and usually provides a good talking point. Red probably lends itself better to this colour scheme than any other hue, but pink can also be used successfully in this way though it is not quite as striking.

Analogous

To explain an analogous colour scheme you really need to picture in your mind a colour wheel. First think of the colours of the rainbow – red, orange, yellow, green, blue, indigo, violet – then put them into a wheel by putting the red next to the violet. To take this a step further, imagine this central circle flanked by an outer circle of the same colours with white added giving the tints and an inner circle with black added to give the shades. In this way an arrangement can be built up on a red, red-orange and orange scheme or a yellow-green, green and blue-green theme and so on. This is a very useful type of colour scheme especially when it

The outline flowers of an apricot-coloured arrangement in a dark green tazza. Three gladioli are the tallest flowers at the top and to make the widest points there is a rose on the left and a carnation spray on the right. The longest flower over the front edge is another carnation spray.

is impossible to obtain shades and tints of one colour. When using this type of scheme try to use the lightest of the colours at the top of the arrangement and also on the widest points as they will show up so much better. One can also go a step further on the colour wheel for this colour scheme and instead of stopping in the group of red, red-orange and orange, go to the next adjacent colour which is yellow. With the yellow-green, green and blue-green you can go to the next adjacent colour which is blue.

The arrangement described here is an example of this type of colour scheme and is in the blue-green range of colours. It is an L-shaped arrangement which would be suitable for a mantelpiece and is in a black oval pottery trough, which has a pinholder in the left-hand corner and wire netting placed over it as explained in Chapter 7. There are nine pale blue delphiniums, five blue irises, two bunches of cornflowers, 12 stems of *Alchemilla mollis*, some green euphorbia, stripped lime and three lime-green hosta

The completed monochromatic arrangement in apricots. It is a basic facing arrangement and the flowers included are roses, gladioli, gerbera, tulips and carnation sprays. The foliage is skimmia and croton leaves.

leaves. These provide a good variety of shape for a mixed flower arrangement. Begin three-quarters of the way back and just in from the left-hand side. Secure a fairly straight piece of lime onto the pinholder. Ideally it should curve towards the left. Place a second shorter stem of lime to the left of the first and close to it. Establish the widest point on the right with a further stem of lime, again securing it three-quarters of the way back in the container. This stem should curve naturally towards the surface on which the trough is standing, and it should be roughly the same length as the tallest lime. A second shorter piece should be placed in front of this one.

Next go back to the top of the arrangement and place a piece of alchemilla close to and shorter than the first lime and to the right-hand side of it. Then position another alchemilla low on the left-hand side. This is the widest point here and it should project a little way over the edge of the trough. It is placed in horizontally, three-quarters of the way back in the container. Flowers will be placed into the

arrangement so that they graduate from the tallest stem to this widest one and so the stem length of this alchemilla should be long enough to accommodate them. A third alchemilla becomes the longest one at the front, in line with the tallest lime at the back. As the trough is narrow it is more important that stems radiate well.

Place a blue delphinium at the back so that it is taller than the tallest lime; a second, shorter delphinium goes to the left of this flower, with a cornflower, a little shorter still, to the right. Place another delphinium close to the widest lime on the right-hand side, a little shorter still. Place another delphinium close to the widest lime on the right-hand side, a little shorter than it. This completes the basic outline, which should not be exceeded.

Next place the blue irises in the centre. Place a long-stemmed and small-flowered one to the left side of the second delphinium at the top, then go to the front edge and place a small-flowered iris to the right of the longest alchemilla at the front. A third iris should be placed in between

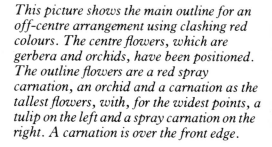

This picture shows the main outline for an off-centre arrangement using clashing red colours. The centre flowers, which are gerbera and orchids, have been positioned. The outline flowers are a red spray carnation, an orchid and a carnation as the tallest flowers, with, for the widest points, a tulip on the left and a spray carnation on the right. A carnation is over the front edge.

these two in the centre of the container. The position of the fourth iris is between the centre and front one but slightly to the right of both and shorter in the arrangement. The fifth and, again, shorter iris is placed between the tallest at the back and the centre one but slightly to the left of both of them. The three hosta leaves frame the irises: a small one goes under the iris at the front edge, another small one goes at the back facing this one with the largest leaf a little to the side and low into the centre. Turn this leaf slightly

sideways. Place some foliage and shorter pieces of alchemilla to cover the netting. Connect up the groups through the centre, and make sure the flowers do not overshadow the outline. Some of the larger flowers can go very short into the arrangement, while having some variation in their length of stem. The left of the arrangement where the height is established is the only place where the flowers can be built out as in a symmetrical facing arrangement. Make sure that the netting is covered at the back.

The clashing red arrangement completed, using orange and red as well as magenta flowers. The grouping and placement of the flowers is as for a basic asymmetrical arrangement. The container is a green pottery bowl, with wire netting and florists' foam underneath the netting.

71

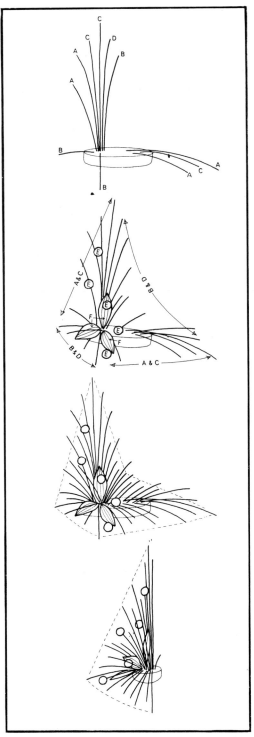

Left and below: An L-shaped arrangement in blues and greens. The line drawings show the main outline points, the placement of the centre flowers and leaves and more outline flowers, how the remaining flowers and foliage are placed, and a side view. The flowers and foliage used are lime (A), alchemilla (B), delphinium (C), cornflower (D), iris (E) and hosta (F).

Complementary

These are the colours which are opposite to each other in the colour wheel and an arrangement using them is most successful when they are of equal intensity, for example, clear red with clear green or apricot with cobalt blue.

Arrangements of one colour with white

Pastel colours are nicer to use with white because they do not provide such a contrast; for this reason red and white are best not seen together, apart from the fact that many people are superstitious about using these particular colours together. Pale yellow and white are pretty together, as are pale pink and white. If using pale blue and white it would be better to use the white on the outline with the blue nearer the centre as blue may not be seen very well against the white on the outline.

Mixed colours

These can be very attractive and can be used in various kinds of arrangements. I have already written about a Dutch group in Chapter 1, where I borrowed the ideas for the colours and flowers from 17th-century Dutch and Flemish flower paintings and created my own Dutch painting. You could copy an actual painting or make your own Dutch group. It is quite

easy now to obtain the flowers of the different seasons as many types are grown in glasshouses.

Another attractive way to use mixed flowers is to make a selection of different coloured flowers from the garden – just one or two of each colour – and arrange them in an appropriate container such as a basket. White flowers can be a little difficult in a mixed coloured arrangement because the eye immediately goes to the white which detracts from the rest, so if you do use them, place them near the centre. Lime-green flowers are excellent with mixed colours; they blend well and lend sharpness to an arrangement. There are many green flowers you can choose, such as *Alchemilla mollis*, lime-green nicotiana, *Amaranthus viridis*, the green zinnia called 'envy', many of the euphorbias, to name just a few. To bring out the colours of other flowers you should include yellow ones. Having different shaped flowers as well as different colours adds extra interest.

Victorian arrangements look specially pleasing in rooms furnished with antiques. The Victorian idea of colour was rather hard and they used bright and gaudy hues. Try to use the flowers which would have been available then such as geraniums and either pack them tightly as they did at the beginning of the period or in an epergne or a piece of Victorian glass with fern for the kind of less full arrangement which they preferred towards the end of the period.

Opposite page: Mixed coloured flowers can be successfully arranged together in various ways. This is an asymmetrical facing arrangement in pastel shades and includes pink and mauve freesia, yellow jasmine, pale green Helleborus foetidus and a blue hyacinth in the centre.

Brightly coloured vases need extra care in choosing the flowers to go in them. As this vase is decorated it is more pleasing to have a simple line arrangement with five red chrysanthemum blooms and Mahonia bealei *leaves. A description of how to prepare the arrangement is given in this chapter.*

Mixed pastel colours are very effective when used with small mixed spring flowers. Flowers which have pretty shades are the pale pink roman hyacinths, primroses, blue muscari, pale green hellebores and pale mauve freesia. These can all be useful for a children's party decoration, especially a girl's party; trails of ribbon can go from the arrangement to each child's place at table with a present on the end. Pastel-coloured flowers look attractive when arranged in a natural way by having clumps of flowers on a dish with bun moss.

Best colours to use for darker rooms

You need to take special care when selecting colour schemes for some buildings such as churches and also rooms which do not get very much light. Certain colours show up so much better than others in poor light, such as yellow and white which reflect light, or orange and flame which both contain some yellow and are good colours to use if the arrangement is to be seen from a distance.

Pinks are not really suitable, but if you are employing them use the salmon-pinks rather than the blue-pinks. This also applies to reds, the yellow-reds being better than the blue-reds. Blue is a very poor colour to use as it absorbs light and will disappear in poor light and change colour in artificial light. It is also better not to use blue at the top of an arrangement when using other colours, as the other colours would be seen but not the blue which would make the arrangement look like it is oddly shaped.

Foliage colour

With any colour scheme of flowers, it is usually possible to obtain a foliage which complements it. With red flowers you can usually get reddish foliage or red-stemmed foliage to blend with them. Pink flowers look well with grey foliage and you can also get some leaves with a pink tinge which pick up the colour of the flower. Grey foliage also blends well with blue flowers as do lime-green coloured leaves. Orange flowers are complemented by leaves tinted and shaded orange and on through the browner shades – glycerined leaves such as beech blend well with these flowers. Yellow flowers are especially good with yellow and lime-green foliage, and white flowers look attractive with lime-green leaves. The foliage belonging to the flowers is always suitable and is, of course, more natural, but adding a foliage colour to match the flowers does give that extra something to an arrangement.

Coloured containers

These can cause problems because of matching the flowers to them. The most useful colour is dull yellow-green, as many different coloured flowers will look well against it. White containers can be rather obvious and create too great a contrast to the colour of the flowers, but these are probably the most easily obtainable in many different shapes. Orange and other brightly coloured containers are occasionally useful but on the whole you will probably find them rather limiting.

Silver and pewter containers are particularly good arranged with whites, pinks, mauves and, for festive occasions, reds. Copper is superb with red or orange flowers and for mixed green flowers and foliage. Brass is excellent with yellow flowers and again a mixed green colouring. Basketwork is better with orange, red and yellow flowers and those of mixed colouring.

This orangy-red narrow-necked vase is made of pottery and has a darker red decoration on it. I chose five red chrysanthemum blooms and nine *Mahonia bealei* leaves, some of which are in the darker red of the markings on the container. As the vase was wide enough at the top, I was able to wedge a piece of florists' foam into it, leaving a space for the water. The container is filled with water as the wieght helps to balance the chrysanthemum blooms as well as keeping the florists' foam wet.

Start off with a long-stemmed small flower, three-quarters of the way back in the centre of the container. Next place a slightly larger but shorter-stemmed flower to the left of the first flower, and a little further forward in the foam. The third flower, a little larger still but shorter-stemmed, is placed to the right of the first flower and again further forward in the foam. The fourth and largest flower, with the shortest stem, is placed a little to the left, fairly low in the arrangement. The fifth flower is fairly small and is placed on the front edge to the right of the centre. These five flowers zig-zag through the arrangement. The mahonia leaves are placed in next, with the darker colours kept nearer the centre. Place one going as high as possible at the back to cover some of the stems of chrysanthemums, and one horizontally on each side, not too wide in keeping with the shape of the container. The longest one in the front is in line with the tallest flower at the back. Arrange the rest of the leaves through the arrangement, some going around the edge and some through with the chrysanthemums, and making sure that the foam is covered.

11 Basic Arrangements

In this chapter the main shapes of arrangements are described; from these shapes derive most other flower arrangements. These are the facing arrangement – symmetrical and asymmetrical – all-round, table centre and L-shape. Each one is described in mixed flowers and also in one variety of flower. The mixed flowers enables one to see how flowers and foliage are grouped as well as how the different shaped flowers and foliage are used.

With any arrangement the plant material and container need to be chosen with care. You will probably not have the identical containers I use, but as long as they are of similar shape and care is taken selecting the flowers and foliage to go into them, you will be successful. The plant material will probably be different from what I am using, but if you get similar shapes and approximately the same amount when you are creating your arrangement, you will find it more challenging and thus far more rewarding. It will help to read Chapter 2 on the general principles of flower arranging before beginning the arrangements.

Facing arrangement in a bowl using mixed flowers

The first arrangement is a symmetrical facing arrangement. The container I have chosen is a green pottery bowl – a vase with a stem, for instance a tazza, would be completed in the same way. In the bowl is a pinholder, placed three-quarters of the way back in the container, with wire netting over it, as explained in Chapter 7. The flowers are in shades of red and are five gladioli, which are pointed flowers, nine stems of single spray chrysanthemum, 11 carnations, three chrysanthemum blooms. The foliage and berries are snowberry leaves, skimmia, cotoneaster leaves and berries, holly foliage, three stems of leycesteria with berries and three bergenia leaves.

With this collection you need to consider where to place the flowers, leaves and berries to make a balanced arrangement. The gladioli and carnations, with

the snowberry and skimmia, one being small-leafed and the other more solid-looking, go through one way. Balancing the other group are the spray chrysanthemum, which has many heads on a stem, and the cotoneaster berries and leaves to assist it, with the holly, again a more solid-looking foliage like the skimmia. The main flowers, the three chrysanthemum blooms, are kept for the centre with the three leycesteria and bergenia leaves.

Begin three-quarters of the way back in the centre with a gladiolus, as this is a tall, light-weight flower. As a rough guide, if you use a vase with a stem, this flower needs to be one-and-a-half times the height of the container, but with a bowl it needs to be about twice the width of the bowl. To the right of the gladiolus place a small-headed chrysanthemum spray; some of the secondary flowers may need to be taken from the stem to make it lighter, and these can be used later to add depth to the arrangement. This flower is a little shorter than the first. On the left side of the gladiolus place a second gladiolus, a little shorter than the spray chrysanthemum. If possible, secure these three flowers in the same hole in the netting and adjacent to each other on the pinholder. This helps to ensure a pointed top to the arrangement.

Next establish the widest points so that the overall width is approximately the same as the height, remembering the grouping, so place the gladiolus on the right side, horizontally on the edge, three-quarters of the way back in the bowl, but making sure it will be in the water. On the opposite side place a small-flowered chrysanthemum spray, if possible with a curved stem so that it arches over the edge. This is not always possible with certain flowers, so curved stems of foliage can be used later, to join the bowl with plant material. All the stems should appear to radiate from the tallest flower. Now the stems demarcating the width have been positioned, place a flower well over the centre front edge of the bowl, in a line with the tallest gladiolus. A small carnation can be used for this. It becomes

Opposite page, top left: The main outline flowers of a basic facing arrangement in red flowers. The container is a green bowl in which there is a pinholder with wire netting over it. The main outline consists of three gladioli, two chrysanthemum sprays and a carnation. Note how the flowers are brought from high on one side to low on the opposite side.

Opposite page, centre left: The second stage of the symmetrical red arrangement where more flowers have been added around the periphery. The main flowers and leaves in the centre, the three chrysanthemum blooms and the three bergenia leaves, have been placed in position. Foliage has been arranged throughout the bowl. Note the grouping, with the gladioli, carnations, snowberry and skimmia foliage going one way and the cotoneaster berries and holly foliage with the chrysanthemum sprays the other.

Opposite page, bottom left: The finished basic facing arrangement of mixed red flowers. Each group of flowers connects through the centre, close to which some leycesteria berries have been placed.

Above: A side view of the basic facing arrangement. Make sure the wire netting at the back of the arrangement is covered.

the longest flower at the front of the arrangement and completes the placement of the main outline flowers, as shown in the first picture. None of the subsequent stems should exceed these in length or the shape of the arrangement will be lost.

The chrysanthemum blooms and bergenia leaves which give heart to the arrangement are positioned next. The large centre flowers should not be in a straight line but should be arranged in a zig-zag fashion. Only three very large centre flowers are being used for this particular arrangement but often five or even seven are incorporated. Although an arrangement needs weight in the centre, the effect should not be too heavy. Place the largest bloom low near the centre with a smaller one above it to the left; the third chrysanthemum bloom goes low on the left front edge. The large leaves are positioned to frame the blooms and an uneven number is again used to prevent the arrangement from appearing too regimented. One bergenia leaf goes over the front edge, one goes at the back facing the one at the front and the largest goes low into the centre and turned slightly sideways.

Proceed by joining up the principal outline flowers around the edge, remembering to keep your flowers in thier groups. The gladioli and carnations extend from high on the left to low on the right and the spray chrysanthemum are arranged in the opposite direction. Bring the stem length down quite sharply at the back to achieve a triangular shape rather than a fan shape and have a good semi-circle around the front edge. Aim for a broken line around the edge with plenty of variation of stem length to prevent the arrangement becoming too set.

On completion of the outline, place in some foliage, keeping the snowberry and skimmia with the gladioli and carnations and the cotoneaster and holly with the chrysanthemum sprays. Follow the line of the flowers through, placing some foliage fairly high and some low to cover the netting. It is easier to fill in with foliage to cover the netting as you progress, rather than waiting until the arrangement is nearly complete.

Next position the three stems of leycesteria berries to add interest in the centre with the blooms and bergenia leaves: one fairly high near the centre, allowing the berries to be seen easily and if necessary removing some of the leaves to achieve this, one over the edge at the front to the right of the longest carnation and, between these two, the third to the left of the centre.

Connect the groups of flowers through the centre so that they merge together,

remembering the general principles of flower arranging as in Chapter 2. When all the flowers are in position, check that the netting is covered including that at the back behind the flowers, so that if the arrangement is seen from the side it will not present an unfinished appearance. The netting can be covered with short pieces of foliage and any short flowers which are surplus. Some longer pieces can be used to cover the stems of the flowers and disguise any stalky effect that might develop. Do not overdo the foliage, however, as this can ruin the whole arrangement. Study the arrangement by standing away from it and making the necessary adjustments. The series of pictures for this arrangement shows how the arrangement is built up to completion and shows a side view of it, too.

Facing arrangement in a vase with a stem using one kind of flower

When arranging one kind of flower, extra care needs to be taken with their placement. The flowers are pink cyclamen and their own foliage is being used. The container is a pink fluted pottery vase with a stem which has florists' foam with netting over it, placed in as explained in Chapter 7.

As with mixed flowers, begin three-quarters of the way back in the centre of the container. A small but tall flower is required, and needs to be at least one-and-a-half times the height of the container. Next position a cyclamen on either side of this first flower, each a slightly different length and each a little larger. Then mark the width, still three-quarters of the way back in the vase, by placing a small flower horizontally on either side. The overall width of the arrangement is approximately the height of it. The longest flower at the front is placed in next and is again a small cyclamen, coming well out over the front edge, and in a line with the tallest flower at the back. This establishes the main outline flowers.

The three largest of the leaves can be placed in next, one going towards the back, one over the front edge to the right of the centre and one placed in sideways in the centre. Go back to the outline and join the principal cyclamen around the periphery – when using one variety of flower you do not need to worry about grouping. Come down quite sharply at the back to keep a triangular shape, and have a semi-circle around the front edge. A broken line is needed around the edge which is achieved with variation of stem length. When the outline is completed, place foliage throughout the arrangement, some leaves going over the edge,

A basic facing arrangement using one kind of flower. These are pink cyclamen with their own leaves, and they are arranged in a pink fluted china vase. Extra care needs to be taken with the placement when using only one kind of flower.

some covering the netting and some placed a little higher. With one kind of flower the only interest is with their placement, so be extra careful with the variation of length and do not have two flowers of the same length side by side. The smaller cyclamen are positioned higher and the larger ones shorter in the arrangement. Keep the weight in the centre. Place some flowers sideways to look more natural. All flower stems should radiate well, and not have their stems crossing. When the flowers are evenly distributed, check that the netting is covered, including the netting at the back of the arrangement.

All-round arrangement in mixed flowers

First I will describe this basic arrangement using mixed flowers. The container is a white pottery bowl with three legs at the base, but any round container could be substituted, whether on a stem or not. In the container is a pinholder placed in the centre with several layers of wire netting over it, as described in Chapter 7. The flowers chosen are five yellow single spray chrysanthemums, five pale yellow double spray chrysanthemums, three stems of apricot spray chrysanthemums, seven stems of yellow spray carnations – the buds of these tend to look spiky – and five orange gerbera. The foliage includes variegated ivy, golden privet, small-leafed berberis and three bergenia leaves.

For an all-round arrangement it is probably easier to establish the shape around the edge first. This is achieved by having an uneven number of outline points. In this arrangement I have seven but a smaller one could have five whereas a larger one may need nine or 11. The more outline points used, within reason, the easier it is to get a good shape. For the outline flowers I have two single yellow spray chrysanthemums, two spray carnations, two double yellow spray chrysanthemums and one apricot spray chrysanthemum. It is preferable to introduce each kind of flower into the outline, although this is not always possible when a particularly short-stemmed variety of flower is being used or when the centre flowers are quite large, as they would be too heavy on the outline with the other flowers being used – as in the case of the gerbera in this arrangement.

The outline flowers chosen should be the smaller ones of each variety, as this keeps the arrangement lighter around the edge. All the outline stems are exactly the same length from the rim of the container to the tip of the flower, in order to ensure that the round shape is kept. They should also be placed roughly the same distance apart. If two of each kind of flower are being used to create the outline, then they should be on opposite sides of the container. However, if fewer varieties of flowers are being used, three of one kind of flower may be needed on the outline. In this case place one flower on one side and two adjacent diagonally opposite. Should the outline contain four of a kind, place two adjacent on one side and the other two diagonally opposite to these. The flower stems go horizontally into the container, about halfway into the centre and below the water line. The flowers should extend well over the edge of the container but not so far as to overpower it. For this size container, which is approximately 150 mm (6 inches) in diameter, about 100 mm (4 inches) over the edge is sufficient. The size of the arrangement is also related to the amount of plant material available, but always allow the flowers to overlap the container; never stop at the rim as this will give a stuffed appearance, and the arrangement will not flow well. All the flowers in an all-round arrangement are aimed towards the centre.

In the case of this arrangement, there is a yellow single spray chrysanthemum one side and one diagonally opposite it, a yellow spray carnation on one side and one diagonally opposite on the other side and the same for the double spray chrysanthemums; there is just one apricot spray chrysanthemum. When these outline flowers are placed in position, the height can be determined. In a basic all-round arrangement the height is approximately the same as the overall width, but sometimes it can be lower depending on what the position the arrangement is to be in a room. The flower chosen to establish the height needs to be small flowered if possible and fairly pointed. This is why a bud of the spray carnation has been chosen, not only because it is small but also because it is light in colour. When the tallest flower has been firmly established in the centre of the pinholder, place flowers of various kinds around close to it. None of them should be as tall and each needs to be a slightly different height. Usually four fairly small flowers are sufficient to create a pretty pointed top to the arrangement. In this case I have used small flowers of apricot spray chrysanthemum, single and double yellow spray chrysanthemums and a spray carnation. The width and height have now been established and none of the subsequent flowers or leaves should go beyond these or the shape will be lost.

Now go back to the outline flowers around the edge of the container and

Below: The first stage in the development of a basic all-round arrangement in a white pottery bowl, showing the main outline flowers. The flowers around the edge are two yellow single chrysanthemum sprays, two yellow spray carnations, two cream double chrysanthemum sprays and one apricot double chrysanthemum spray. The tallest flower in the centre is a small spray carnation with the other kinds of flowers introduced around it.

Above: The second stage of the basic all-round arrangement shows more flowers placed between the outline edges. The main flowers, the gerbera, and the main leaves, the bergenia, have been placed fairly near the centre, and some foliage is also in position.

Above right: This picture shows the completed basic all-round arrangement. Its height is approximately the same as its overall width.

place flowers of varying lengths in between them. Some need to be practically as long as the main outline flowers, but do not cut them all exactly the same length as you will obtain a circle within a circle. A less set pattern is more attractive. Conversely, if these flowers are cut too short and placed against the rim of the bowl, a star-shaped arrangement will be created and not a round one. It is advisable when making the all-round arrangement to keep turning the container round, otherwise the tendency is to complete one side and not have sufficient flowers left for the other side, resulting in an unbalanced arrangement. A cake icing turntable is very useful to use when doing an all-round arrangement. The main flowers through the centre of the bowl can be positioned next – these are the gerbera. One is placed near to the outline edge on either side of the arrangement, one comes fairly high near the centre group of flowers and the other two in lower on either side, again zig-zagging them across the container. The three bergenia leaves are placed one on one side, another on the opposite side, and one near the centre turning sideways, but not in a line with the other two. Some of the foliage can be placed through, keeping each variety grouped together.

The grouping of the flowers should run from one side to the diagonally opposite side, keeping each kind of flower as established in the main outline. Where only one flower is in the main outline still take some flowers through to the diagonally opposite side but not quite as far as the main outline flowers. When looking down from above the arrangement, however, the flowers should not be in straight lines across the bowl but should zig-zag across to the opposite side. A flower group should merge with the group next to it, that is, the spray carnations can have a few flowers in with the apricot chrysanthemum spray, so that the arrangement does not look too set. Remember to have variation of stem length and keep in mind the other general principles of flower arranging.

The rest of the foliage can be placed in now, grouped through as for the flowers, with some placed low to cover any netting which can be seen. Finally turn the arrangement around and check that the flowers and foliage is correctly placed. The three pictures show how the all-round bowl was created.

All-round arrangement of one kind of flower

As with the facing arrangement with one variety of flower, here you do not need to worry about the grouping of the flowers. These are daffodils and of the variety 'fortune'; the foliage is variegated privet and the leaves of the daffodils.

Daffodils are used for a basic all-round arrangement of one kind of flower in a wicker basket with a handle. The first stage shows the seven outline points established around the edge and the tallest flowers positioned in the centre. The second stage shows how more flowers of various lengths have been added between the outline points and the variegated privet placed into the arrangement. The picture of the completed arrangement shows how the flowers are built up from the outline flowers to the centre.

Opposite page, top: The main outline points of a basic table centre in a lined silver cake basket with a handle. The flowers are all pink, with a tulip the longest flower on one side and a carnation the longest on the opposite side. There are three flowers of different lengths at either end and they are grouped diagonally across the container. Hyacinths establish the widest points on the sides and they provide the main flower in the centre as well as the tallest.

The container chosen is a round wicker basket with a handle. Some baskets have a watertight lining when bought, but if it has not you can usually find a container to fit the basket. I found a cake tin in the cupboard which fitted perfectly. If the lining container goes too deeply into the basket, you can put some padding into the basket to lift the inner container level with the rim of the basket. Into the centre of the tin I placed a pinholder with wire netting over it, as explained in Chapter 7, and tied it into the tin with reel wire as you would a parcel. I chose the basket as it is a rural-looking container in keeping with the flowers. When arranging a handled basket, part of the handle should be seen in the completed arrangement.

For this size basket, seven outline points are required as for the mixed all-round. These points should be approximately the same distance apart all the way around the container and the same length from the edge of the basket to the tip of the daffodil trumpet. Use the smaller blooms for the edge. Place the tallest daffodil in the centre, this being quite a small flower, and place two or three flowers around it, each a different length and each a little shorter than the first flower. These are all placed quite close together on the pinholder. Radiate stems towards the tallest flower in the centre.

Position more flowers of varying lengths horizontally around the outline between the principal outline points.

Then place in some of the privet foliage, around the outline and going through the container to cover some of the netting, and going higher into the arrangement. Some of the daffodil spikes can be placed in bunches of threes and fives as these tend to look better than placing them in singly. Do not have them too long and group them through the basket in a zigzag fashion.

Keep turning the basket around and place the remaining daffodils into the arrangement, some going in very short, and some beneath the handle. Also have some building up to the tallest flower from the outline edge so that a triangular shape is formed. Distribute the daffodils equally around the basket. Finish by placing in more foliage through with the flowers and low to cover the netting. Finally stand away from the arrangement to make sure the plant material is in the right position and that part of the handle is visible.

Table centre in mixed flowers

These arrangements can be created in trough-shaped containers and in oblong and oval dishes often from the kitchen. They can be on a stem but this could make them too high for the centre of a table. The container I have selected is an oval silver cake basket with a handle. Inside it, used as a lining, is a glass pie dish, in the centre of which is placed a pinholder which has several layers of wire netting placed over it, as explained in

Chapter 7. Use florists' foam if preferred, either on its own or a piece placed under the netting instead of a pin-holder. The netting is attached to the handle of the basket on both sides with reel wire to hold the dish in position.

The flowers and foliage chosen to go with the silver container are in shades of pink with grey foliage. They are 13 dark pink tulips, nine darker-pink-flecked carnations and five stems of pink hyacinth. Hyacinth keep quite well when cut and

Above: The completed pink table centre. The flowers used are 15 tulips with Senecio greyii *foliage grouped one way, and seven carnations with santolina foliage the other. Five hyacinths are placed through the centre with ivy leaves.*

are a different shaped flower so add interest to an arrangement. They also come in attractive colours which match well with a variety of other flowers. The grey foliage is *Senecio greyii*, which has small leaves on a stem, santolina, which is a feathery type of foliage, and five large grey-green variegated ivy leaves tinged with pink.

With a table centre it is perhaps easier to begin with the flowers which mark the length of the arrangement, where possible using the smaller flowers and those with curved stems so that the plant material becomes linked with the container. Various factors, including the size of the container, will determine how far these stems should project over the edge of the container. The projection, however, should be the same on either side. On the left side place two tulips and one carnation; the smallest tulip is the longest; the second tulip, about half a head shorter than the first, is placed to one side of it and on the other side of it the carnation, about half a head shorter again. These go fairly close together, but if the container was narrower, they would be closer together in keeping with the shape of the container. Next go to the right side of the container and place two carnations and one tulip here. The smaller carnation is the longest one, and on one side of this the second carnation is placed diagonally opposite the carnation on the left side of the silver basket. The tulip is placed on the side of the longest carnation, diagonally opposite to the second tulip on the left. Again the three flowers on the right are about half a head shorter than each other and placement is the same as for the three on the opposite end.

All these stems should appear to radiate from the centre of the container, but they do not reach as far as the pinholder. Secure them into the wire netting. The widest point on either side is marked by two fairly small-flowered hyacinth, which need to be far enough over the edge so that you can build out from the ends to the sides though they are not as long as the flowers on the ends. Take into consideration the oval shape of the container and try and keep this shape. As the container is a basket with a handle, one hyacinth goes on one side of the handle on one side and the other hyacinth goes on the opposite side of the handle on the other side. They would be directly opposite if it was a container without a handle. It is better to introduce each kind of flower on the outline if at all possible.

The height is established by a hyacinth, as it is a pointed flower and so gives a lightness to the arrangement at the top. This is placed through the netting onto the pinholder. As this is a table centre the height should not obscure the view of anyone across the table. These outline flowers are shown in the first picture of the arrangement. Next place in two or three flowers – tulips and carnations – around the centre hyacinth, quite close to it but all shorter and with varying lengths. Where possible introduce each kind of flower around the centre flower. Return to the edge of the container and connect up the main outline flowers, having a broken line. Keep the grouping in the right position, going diagonally across the container. As with an all-round arrangement it is an advantage to keep turning the container round, to ensure that the flowers are distributed evenly.

As the hyacinth are the main flowers, and there are only five of them, they should be positioned near the centre. Three have been used already, and the other two should now be placed between the widest one and the tallest one on either side, so that they zig-zag across. Cover the netting with some foliage and also place some out over the edge of the container, but keeping it within the main outline points. The *Senecio greyii* is grouped with the carnations, and the santolina with the tulips. The five leaves are kept near the centre with the hyacinth, one coming out on each side of the silver basket under the hyacinth, one in the centre, and between the side and centre one on either side. These are fairly short in the arrangement.

Connect the flower groups through the arrangement with as much variation of stem length as possible, having the larger flowers in shorter, the smaller higher. A few tulip leaves, which have been removed from the tulip, can be used by rolling a short piece of their stem in the bottom of the leaf, which helps it to stay in position in the netting more easily. Keep the tulip leaves grouped with the tulip flowers. Merge the groups of flowers together through the centre. Check that the wire netting is covered and that the flowers are well distributed.

Table centre using one kind of flower

When you use one type of flower, you need to concentrate on the shape, variation of length and where to place the different sized flowers.

This container is an oval trough in white pottery and has a pinholder in the centre with wire netting over it, placed in as described in Chapter 7. The flowers being used are yellowy gerbera or Barbeton daisies and the foliage chosen is croton

A basic table centre of gerbera with croton and bergenia leaves in a white pottery trough. The weight in the centre is achieved with bergenia leaves. Three flowers are placed at either end and one on either side to provide the main outline. The yellow of the croton leaves picks up the colouring of the gerbera.

leaves and the single leaves of bergenia which add interest to the centre of the arrangement.

The main outline flowers are placed in first, three on either end of the container and each a different length, the centre one of the three being the longest. The tallest gerbera in the centre is a small flower and is not too high, and has two or three flowers of different lengths around it. Next place more gerbera around the outline edge in a broken line, and keep the shape already established with the main outline flowers. Place some croton foliage in next, around the edge and covering some of the netting. The large bergenia leaves are placed through the centre from one side edge of the container to the other. Place flowers throughout the arrangement, keeping the larger ones in lower especially near the centre. Gradually build up higher from the ends and widest points to the tallest gerbera in the centre. Check that the netting is covered and that foliage is placed to cover some of the flower stems. It is especially important with one kind of flower that they are evenly spaced through the arrangement.

L-shaped arrangement using one kind of flower

L-shaped arrangements can be placed in trough-type containers, oval dishes and lidded baskets. Containers with stems are not usually suitable for them.

For this L-shaped arrangement I have used a lidded basket which has a rustic look and in keeping with this I have chosen a collection of chrysanthemum sprays in three shades, so even though there is only one type of flower being used, the grouping can be seen by the coloured chrysanthemum. If only one colour is being used it would be arranged in a similar way. There are six stems of yellow and four stems of bronze single spray chrysanthemums, and two stems of double bronze spray chrysanthemums. The double bronze chrysanthemum is the largest variety being used and is therefore an excellent choice for the main flower in the centre to give the weight. As the chrysanthemum are the spray kind, many of the secondary flowers can be taken from the main stem and used individually, which makes them an economical choice. The foliage is two varieties of cotoneaster and three leaves of *Mahonia*

aquifolia for the centre with the largest flowers.

The basket has a plastic lining, and in this is a small pinholder on the left-hand side about three-quarters of the way back a little way in from the side, where the tallest flowers will be placed. Wire netting is placed in the lining over the pinholder, as described in Chapter 7. L-shaped arrangements are useful in lidded baskets, as part of the lid needs to be kept free.

Begin three-quarters of the way back, and just in from the left-hand side. Secure a small and fairly straight-stemmed flower of the yellow single spray chrysanthemum. I use yellow in preference to bronze as, being of a lighter colour, it is more noticeable. To the right of this, a little shorter, is a fairly small bronze single spray chrysanthemum, and on the left, again a little shorter, a yellow single chrysanthemum, each of these two flowers being progressively larger. These three flowers are quite close together with the stems going into the netting and secured into the pinholder. Next go to the right-hand side of the basket and place a small yellow chrysanthemum three-quarters of the way back in the

A lidded basket is used for the basic L-shaped arrangement of chrysanthemum sprays in three colours. The first picture shows the main outline flowers, four yellow and two bronze single chrysanthemum sprays. The outline flower on the right side is longer than that on the left, thus forming the L shape. The second picture shows the

completed arrangement with the single yellow chrysanthemum spray and one variety of cotoneaster going from high on the left to low on the right, and the bronze single chrysanthemum spray and another variety of cotoneaster going the opposite way. The double bronze chrysanthemum spray is placed as the main flower in the centre.

basket going horizontally into it. The length of it needs to be fairly long to achieve an L with the tallest flower, and make sure it is under the water line. Curved stems should be used if they are available as they connect with the container more easily, but if they are not then use curved foliage for this purpose later. Go to the left side and, still in the same line, place a bronze single chrysanthemum horizontally over the edge of the basket but not as long as for the right side in order to maintain the L shape. The stem length needs to be just long enough for the flowers to graduate from the tallest stem to the widest one. The last flower to be placed in for the principal outline points is a yellow chrysanthemum over the front of the basket in a line with the tallest flower at the back. All the stems should radiate from the tallest stem. The outline flowers are shown in the first picture.

Position the largest flowers, the double bronze chrysanthemums, next. Five of these are sufficient. A fairly small one goes quite high near the tallest three flowers, another fairly small one going over the front edge to the right of the longest flower here. A third fairly long-stemmed flower is placed near the centre and the other two, the largest flowers, go in quite low, so that the five flowers form

a zig-zag pattern through the centre. Place the three mahonia leaves so that they frame these flowers: a piece over the front edge, one towards the back and one near the centre.

Position some of the cotoneaster foliage next, around the edge and close to the netting, grouping one cotoneaster with the yellow chrysanthemum and the other with the bronze single chrysanthemum. Then connect up the groups of yellow and bronze flowers, having the single yellow chrysanthemum sprays high on the left to low on the right and the single bronze spray chrysanthemums in the opposite direction. Make sure that the flowers are kept low on the right of the basket at the back, to enable the L-shape to be seen and also to keep the flowers free from that part of the lid. The only part of the arrangement where the flowers can come up fairly high is where the tallest flowers are established on the left. Distribute the plant material as evenly as possible and remember the general principles of flower arranging as explained in Chapter 2. Check that the mechanics of the arrangement are covered and cannot be seen either from the front or the side of the arrangement.

L-shaped arrangement of mixed plant materials

This is an L-shaped arrangement using leaves and flowers in mixed green colouring. The container is a mirror trough, that is, a metal container with mirror glass attached to the sides which will reflect the plant material. It has a pinholder in the left-hand side and is fitted with wire netting, as explained in Chapter 7. These arrangements are especially welcome on very hot days as they give an illusion of coolness, as well as keeping exceptionally well. Attractive results can also be achieved with only foliage, providing a good variety of shape, shade and texture is used.

An ideal position for this arrangement would be a mantelpiece with a mirror over it, so that the arrangement is framed in half of the mirror. The plant material includes pointed flag iris leaves, the more solid leaf of elaeagnus, ivy, *Helleborus corsicus* flowers, sedum, the round head of angelica, bitty woad, *Stachys lanata*, *Begonia* 'Iron Cross' with its interesting markings, bright green euphorbia, *Cassinia fulvida*, variegated rue and apple mint, large plain green hosta leaves and lime-green nicotiana. The arrangement is created as for the lidded basket. For the height use a flag iris leaf, securing it three-quarters of the way back in the container. A second flag iris leaf is placed

a little to the right of the first and shorter. A stem of elaeagnus, shorter than the second flag iris leaf, is placed to the opposite side of the tallest leaf. The widest point on the left-hand side, still three-quarters of the way back in the trough, was established with a piece of apple mint and on the right-hand side a stem of euphorbia. A piece of woad becomes the longest stem at the front, in a line with the tallest leaf at the back. I grouped the elaeagnus, rue, ivy, hellebores, sedum and euphorbia high on the left to low on the right and the rest of the plant material the opposite way with the exception of the angelica head, begonia and hosta which I have in the centre. It is more difficult to get the effect of variation of stem length with foliage so I emphasized this aspect with flowers. Be careful, however, to keep the L-shape by making the stems at the right back very short. All the stems again radiate from the tallest one at the back. Have flowers coming around the front edge from the widest points to the longest one at the front. As the container is longer than the lidded basket, the L-shape needs to be more slender. Keep a broken line along the edge so that it does not look too trimmed. Check that all the netting is hidden including that at the back of the mirror trough.

Asymmetrical or off-centre facing arrangement in mixed flowers

This arrangement could be described as a cross between the basic facing and the L-shaped. The tallest flower is not central but about a quarter of the way from

Mixed foliage and a few green flowers are used for the basic L-shaped arrangement in a mirror trough. The grouping is high on one side and low on the opposite side. Extra care needs to be taken when using mainly foliage to ensure that it is not too flat.

either the right- or left-hand side of the arrangement, depending on where the finished arrangement is to be situated. A variety of containers could be used, although baskets and boxes with lids should be avoided and the urn shape, being tall and slender, does not show flowers to their best advantage.

I have selected a collection of pink flowers and some twiggy branches. The flowers are nine stems of kaffir lilies (*Schizostylis coccinea*), four stems of pink spray carnations, three gerbera (Barbeton or Transvaal daisy) and five twigs of *Viburnum fragrans*. The foliage is in grey – hebe, rue, santolina and *Senecio greyii* with three large ivy leaves tinged with pink.

I have chosen a pewter tankard, which is not too high. Containers such as tazzas, bowls and oval containers with or without stems are all suitable. The pewter tankard goes well with the colouring of the flowers and also with their size. In the pewter container only wire netting has been used, as described in Chapter 7, because the tankard is quite deep and therefore it is unnecessary to use a pinholder. However, florists' foam could be used instead.

Begin with the outline flowers three-quarters of the way back in the container and a quarter of the way from the left-hand side, having the handle on this side so that the tallest flower goes up from the handle. Use a twig of viburnum as the longest stem, letting it curve slightly to the left. A second shorter stem of viburnum is positioned to the left of this, curving in line with the first. These stems should be close together to obtain a reasonably pointed shape at the top. A long-stemmed spray carnation which is at the bud stage is placed on the other side of the first viburnum, a little shorter than the second viburnum and close to the first twig, curving to the right. To define the width on the right side place another viburnum twig, longer than the left side, with the stem projecting well over the edge of the container with a downward curve to help give it the illusion of flowing out of the tankard. A small spray carnation is used to mark the widest point on the left-hand side. Place it curving downwards, just behind the handle and shorter than the right-hand side twig. The longest flower over the front edge, in a line with the tallest viburnum, is another viburnum twig.

Use the gerbera and large ivy leaves to give weight and interest in the centre of the pewter tankard. Position the smallest gerbera fairly high at the back, turning slightly, the next smallest over the right front edge and the largest to the left of these two, to avoid having them in a straight line. Place the three ivy leaves to frame the gerbera, one under the gerbera at the front edge, one under the centre gerbera and the third towards the back of the arrangement as shown in the second picture.

Fill in between the main outline flowers, grouping the kaffir lilies with the viburnum high on the left to low on the right and the spray carnations in the opposite direction. Bring the kaffir lilies

The basic asymmetrical facing arrangement in a pewter tankard is shown in three stages of development. The first is the outline shape, achieved with the Viburnum fragrans *and pink spray carnations. At the second stage the outline has been filled in by introducing the kaffir lilies with the viburnum, and positioning the centre flowers, the gerbera, and the centre leaves, the pink-tinged ivy. The third picture shows the completed arrangement, with the flowers connected through the centre and the hebe, rue, santolina and* Senecio greyii *foliage grouped through with the flowers. Make sure that the handle of the tankard is visible.*

In the white china cornucopia is a basic asymmetrical arrangement of white marguerites and small variegated hosta leaves. The outline shape is achieved with the smaller flowers or buds, the larger flowers being placed nearer the centre to give added weight.

the placement of each flower is critical to achieving a result which is completely satisfactory.

The container is a cornucopia or horn of plenty. Often these containers are fashioned in basketwork when they look lovely holding an arrangement of autumn berries and leaves. This one is made of white china so a simple arrangement of marguerites is ideal, the white of the flowers picking up the white of the china and their clear yellow centres adding an air of freshness.

The only leaves used here are the very small ones of *Hosta undulata* which are variegated with creamy white. I chose the clean-cut leaf to keep the clean lines of the arrangement. It is unnecessary to use a pinholder or florists' foam under the netting as the container is sufficiently deep. The netting is fitted as explained in Chapter 7.

Position the outline flowers first with the tallest, fairly small flower in from the edge on the more upright left side of the cornucopia and three-quarters of the way back. The length of the stem is between one and a half and twice the height of the container. Choose a relatively small flower for this; a bud could be used but a flower gives a more definite colour in this circumstance. Place a second slightly larger flower about a head shorter to the right of this and a third flower, again a head shorter, on the opposite side. The widest flower on the right-hand side is a bud but showing some colour, placed so that it flows well out over the edge, and on the left-hand side is another bud, the stem being about half the length of the one on the opposite side. These should both be placed horizontally into the cornucopia. The longest flower over the front edge is in a line with the tallest one at the back. Choosing curved stems to go around the front edge is not difficult when using flowers such as marguerites. This makes them join gracefully with the container.

Fill in the outline, turning some flowers sideways and forming a broken line. It is especially necessary to place some sideways when using flowers with flat faces as it prevents the arrangement looking too set, and gives a more natural appearance. Position some of the leaves, then bring more marguerites through the arrangement. Place the flowers reasonably evenly throughout, the buds and smaller flowers higher and the larger flowers lower, particularly in the centre.

Check that the wire netting is completely covered, not forgetting the back of the cornucopia. Stand away from the arrangement to see if the placement is satisfactory.

high with the viburnum to add more colour. One side of the triangular shape will be longer than the other in this arrangement, and the stems should be decreased quite sharply at the back to avoid a fan shape. Again, as with all arrangements, a broken line is aimed for with plenty of variation of stem length. The front should be reasonably rounded, though one side will be longer than the other, and the flowers near the handle should be shorter so as not to hide it.

Use foliage to go through the arrangement and to cover the netting, the *Senecio greyii* and rue going with the kaffir lilies, and the hebe and santolina with the spray carnations. Connect the flower groups, placing in more flowers throughout the arrangement. Have a good variation of stem length and space the flowers evenly. Remember the general principles of flower arrangement. Finally check that all the netting is covered including that at the back of the pewter tankard, and that the handle can be easily seen.

Asymmetrical arrangement of one kind of flower

This is again an off-centre facing arrangement but this time with one variety of flower. This always appears to be an easier arrangement as the grouping does not have to be considered, only the shape and variation of stem lengths, but in fact when only one variety and colour is used

12 Adaptation of Basic Arrangements

This arrangement of anemones needs to be wider and lower than a basic facing arrangement in consideration of the shape of the shell container. The mauve anemones and santolina foliage are grouped one way and the purple anemones and the Senecio greyii *foliage the opposite way. The large ivy leaves are placed in the centre. A description can be found in this chapter.*

The basic arrangements in Chapter 11 can be adapted to other shaped containers. This chapter begins by describing the various ways this can be achieved and, later, the different shaped arrangements which can be placed in one container.

You can adapt a basic facing arrangement in a bowl or tazza to an urn quite easily. As the shape of the urn is narrower the arrangement needs to be tall and slender, creating a more elegant effect. Whereas for a basic facing arrangement in a bowl or tazza the height is roughly the overall width, for an urn it is usually narrower, the flowers being one and a half to twice the height of the container. An urn can be arranged with mixed flowers, as with the mixed red flowers in the urn in Chapter 5, page 36; or with a few flowers like the arrangement here of five chrysanthemum blooms, three large bergenia leaves and peony foliage in a bronze urn. The chrysanthemum are apricot in colour and the peony leaves have turned to an attractive bronze. As an alternative to the peony leaves you could use preserved beech leaves, which would be brown. When flowers are very large you need a heavy container to balance their weight, which is why I chose an urn on a base.

In the container is a well-soaked piece of florists' foam with wire netting over it. Position the chrysanthemums first, beginning with the smallest flower, the

The five chrysanthemum blooms, peony foliage and three bergenia leaves in a bronze urn require an adaptation of the basic facing arrangement in a tazza. Taller and more slender, the adaptation is described in this chapter.

stem of which was cut so that when secured it is twice the height of the container. This is placed three-quarters of the way back in the centre. A second small chrysanthemum is placed over the front edge of the urn a little to the right. Next position the third, slightly larger flower with a shorter stem to the left of

the first flower leaving a small space between the two blooms. The fourth chrysanthemum, a little larger and shorter-stemmed still, goes to the other side of the first flower. The fifth and largest chrysanthemum is positioned to the side of the fourth flower and short into the arrangement. The stems from the back bloom to the front one are secured a little further forward in the netting.

The three bergenia leaves are placed so that one is over the front edge on the left side to balance the bloom on the right side. The second is towards the back and facing towards the front leaf and the third and largest is placed in low on the opposite side of the urn to the fifth chrysanthemum and is turned sideways.

The peony leaves mark the width but keep them relatively short to enhance the shape of the urn. Place a peony leaf in the front of the container between the bloom and the bergenia leaf to mark the longest point at the front. More peony leaves are positioned attractively through the container and also over the netting.

You can also adapt the basic facing arrangement to low and wide containers such as the shell. This type of container needs the flowers and foliage to be lower in height and wider, in fact a more spreading arrangement. The white china shell in the picture contains mauve and purple anemones. Anemones are often sold in mixed coloured bunches and you could, of course, use the red and white ones too, but if you can find a use for them in another arrangement, it is more attractive to use just the two shades. The foliage is grey, with the santolina going through with the mauve flowers, the *Senecio greyii* going through with the purple flowers, and three large ivy leaves placed near the centre. The arrangement is as for the basic facing arrangement but the tallest flower is kept much lower and the side flowers are much longer. The width is almost twice the height. You still need to begin three-quarters of the way back in the container and the grouping is achieved in the same way. Remember that the general principles of flower arrangement still apply.

With an all-round arrangement, the proportions in a basic arrangement are that the height is roughly the overall width, but this can vary according to the position the arrangement is to be placed in a room. If it is to be used as a table centre it needs to be lower in the centre, and has to be adapted accordingly. When an all-round arrangement is in a candle cup on a candlestick, this also needs to be lower, as the candle gives the height and the rest of the flowers need to be much flatter, but it still needs variation of stem length, as arranged in the brass candlestick in Chapter 4, page 31.

A basic table centre can be adapted to the shape of the container; in one which is oval the three flowers at the ends can be much further apart, in fact making it more of a cross between an all-round and

a table centre. If the container is quite narrow then the first three flowers at each end are very close together in order to keep the shape of the container. If arranging a basket with a high handle then the flowers should be kept underneath it or it would be too high for a table centre.

L-shaped arrangements need not have a mass of flowers but can be adapted to a simple line arrangement on a dish or plate. The black pottery dish is arranged as a line arrangement but, as can be seen, the basic shape is an L. The dish is quite deep so it will hold sufficient water for the flowers. A pinholder is placed on the dish about three-quarters of the way back and just in from the right-hand side. The flowers are nine dark pink roses; in an arrangement such as this it is important to have an uneven number of flowers. The only foliage used is the rose leaves.

Place a small rose on the pinholder, three-quarters of the way back, a slightly

This line arrangement on a pinholder in a black pottery trough using nine roses is explained in detail in this chapter. It is adapted from the basic L-shaped arrangement. Only rose leaves are used with the roses and because of the simplicity of the arrangement some pebbles have been placed in the dish to give added charm.

93

larger flower about a head shorter on the left of this, and coming slightly forward on the pinholder, and the third flower, again shorter, coming forward on the pinholder. Next place in the side flowers on the left-hand side to mark the widest point at this side; the rose stems here are placed sideways on the pinholder. Have a small flower as the longest rose just going over the edge of the container, then position a slightly shorter-stemmed rose on the right of this flower and a third rose on the opposite side, again shorter, and raised up towards the centre of the arrangement. Some leaves can be placed in at this stage to cover some of the pinholder and to establish the widest point on the right-hand side, which comes a short distance from the dish. Wherever possible, keep a small piece of the main rose stem with the leaf. Position the last three roses; the largest goes in fairly short near the centre and the other two are placed on either side of it. As can be seen from the completed arrangement the flowers zig-zag from side to side. Place more leaves attractively through with the roses. Finish by placing some pebbles into the dish to add extra interest as it is a simple arrangement. These go towards the centre, and can help cover some of the pinholder.

Off-centre facing (asymmetrical) arrangements, when placed in certain containers such as a flat shell or a cupid or dolphin which has a shell on it, need to be arranged in a low spreading way in keeping with the container.

Some containers are more useful than others because several different shaped arrangements can be satisfactory placed in them. If you are just beginning flower arranging and do not wish to spend too much money on vases it would be a good idea to start with those which you can do more than one shape in. For a good variety, for both formal and informal arrangements, the containers which would prove most useful are a tazza, a bowl and a trough.

The tazza or a bowl on a stem is better than an urn because the wider top makes it possible to do an all-round arrangement as well as symmetrical and asymmetrical facing arrangements. The bowl is useful as it is suitable for an all-round, a facing – both symmetrical and asymmetrical – and, if the bowl is shallow enough, a line arrangement. The trough is the most versatile of the three as it can be arranged as a table centre, a facing – symmetrical and asymmetrical – an L-shaped and a line arrangement.

For the tazza I am using a small silver vase which is a bowl with a stand of three dolphins. The bowl is a green pottery one

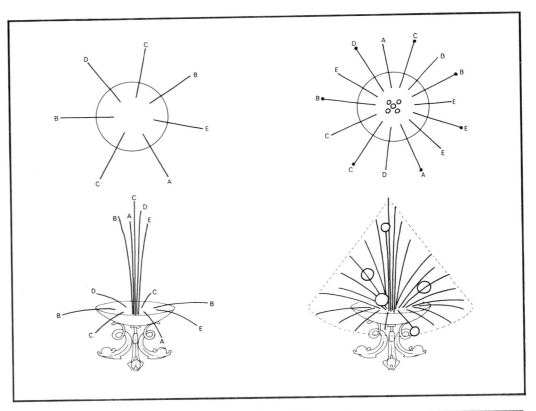

which is quite shallow so a line arrangement can be completed in it, and the trough is a rectangular shallow ovenware dish. If larger containers of the various shapes are required, arrange them in a similar way but with larger flowers.

Here the silver dolphin vase is arranged as an all-round arrangement. As it is silver I have placed in it a small container to

Above: The completed all-round arrangement in the silver dolphin tazza in pink, blue and mauve. With the flowers are leaves of zebrina, variegated ivy and a small variety of saxifrage. This tazza is useful for other shaped arrangements, as can be seen with the symmetrical facing arrangement on page 35 and the asymmetrical facing arrangement on page 73.

Opposite page, top: Line drawings illustrating the development of an all-round arrangement in a small silver tazza. The seven outline points are shown in the first diagram. The second shows the outline points with the centre flower and flowers of different lengths positioned around it. The third diagram indicates the placement of flowers between the main outline points around the edge of the container. The overall shape of the arrangement is illustrated in the fourth diagram. The flowers are roses (A), pussy willow (B), freesia (C), grape hyacinth (D) and ranunculus (E).

Below: This green pottery bowl holds a facing arrangement in green plant material which includes broom, heather, Boston fern (Nephrolepis), *asparagus fern, periwinkle* (Vinca), *scindapsus leaves, parlour palm* (Chamaedorea elegans) *and* Helleborus foetidus. *The method of arranging it is described in this chapter. This bowl can be used for other shaped arrangements, as can be seen on pages 24, 32 and 71.*

hold florists' foam or a pinholder with wire netting over it, whichever is preferred. The flowers are pink, blue and mauve, and include five garnette roses of the variety 'Carol', 15 grape hyacinth (*Muscari*), 11 freesia in pink and mauve, seven pieces of pussy willow and five pink ranunculuses. The foliage is grey-green and mauve colours, and is zebrina, variegated ivy and a small variety of saxifrage.

The all-round arrangement is as for a basic all-round. The main outline points are a rose, two freesia, one grape hyacinth, two pussy willow and one ranunculus. The tallest flower is a pink freesia and is in the centre of the vase, and other flowers of varying lengths of stem are introduced around it. Place more flowers of differing lengths around the outline edge, place some foliage through the arrangement, keeping them in their groups, and then connect up the various groups with flowers throughout the arrangement. On page 35 there is a facing ar-

rangement in this container and on page 73 an asymmetrical arrangement, to show the various ways the container can be used.

The small green pottery bowl is arranged as a facing arrangement, but it is kept lower in the centre, though still having variation of stem length. In the container is a round of florists' foam. The arrangement is mainly of foliage but some *Helleborus foetidus* flowers are used in the centre. The spiky top is achieved by placing in broom, with asparagus fern on its right and heather (erica) on its left. These also mark the widest points, with the asparagus on the left and the heather on the right. The longest leaf over the front edge is a Boston fern (*Nephrolepis*). Grouped with the asparagus fern is periwinkle (*Vinca*) and with the heather the Boston fern. In the centre are three scindapsus leaves, three parlour palm (*Chamaedorea elegans*) and *Helleborus foetidus*. On page 71 this pottery bowl is arranged as an asymmetrical arrangement, on page

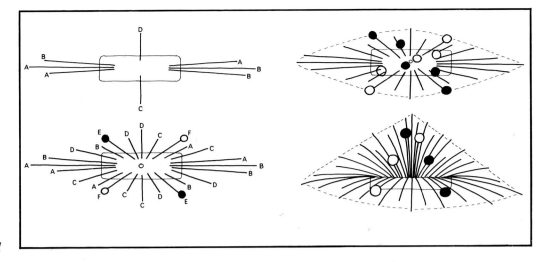

Above right: Line drawings to show in stages how to achieve the table centre in the brown ovenware dish which is described in this chapter. The grouping goes diagonally across the arrangement and the flowers used are montbretia (A), hypericum (B), single spray chrysanthemum (C), double spray chrysanthemum (D) and two kinds of dahlias (E and F). The first three line drawings show a plan view of the arrangement, the main outline being shown in the first one. In the second other flowers are placed between the main outline points, and the tallest one in the centre is positioned. The main flowers in the centre are shown in the third diagram and the fourth shows the overall shape of the arrangement.

Right: This picture shows the completed table centre in the brown ovenware dish in apricot colourings. This trough can also be used for other shaped arrangements. On page 59 it holds a symmetrical facing arrangement, on page 72 an L-shape, on page 47 an asymmetrical facing and on page 37 a line arrangement.

24 as an all-round arrangement, and on page 32 as a line arrangement.

A table centre of apricot and orange shades, including berries for an autumnal arrangement, is in a rectangular brown oven-ware dish. There is a small square of florists' foam in the centre with wire netting over it. The plant material includes 15 montbretia, nine stems of hypericum berries, three berried sprays of viburnum and three of berberis, two stems of single and three stems of double chrysanthemum sprays, five each of two kinds of dahlia, three physalis (Chinese lanterns) seedheads, nine apricot-coloured peony leaves, three sprays of autumnal azalea leaves and five pieces of epimedium.

Place in the plant material for the longest points at each end first. The longest flower on the left is montbretia with a hypericum on one side of it and a montbretia on the other side. The longest piece on the right is a stem of hypericum berries with a montbretia on one side of it, so that it is diagonally opposite the montbretia at the opposite end, and a hypericum on the other side. The tallest flower

in the centre is a bud of double chrysanthemum, with other flowers of different lengths around it. The grouping is single spray chrysanthemums, montbretia, azalea, berberis and viburnum one way and double chrysanthemum sprays, hypericum, Chinese lanterns and peony foliage the opposite way. Dahlias are kept near the centre with one kind each way across the centre. A facing arrangement (symmetrical) is arranged in this trough on page 59, an asymmetrical on page 47, an L-shape on page 72 and a line arrangement on page 37.

Some baskets are quite adaptable to certain shapes, the handled basket more so than the lid. The basket with a handle can be arranged as a facing arrangement and as table centre. You can also turn the basket so that, instead of being placed squarely, it can be corner-ways on and a facing arrangement done in this position. The lid basket can only have facing arrangements in it, but this can be achieved with the tallest flower in the centre leaving the two corners free, or as an L-shape and also with the lid almost closed with the flowers emerging from under it.

13 Just a Few Flowers

Often when only using a few flowers they are placed on a pinholder in a line arrangement, as has already been mentioned in earlier chapters. This is not to be confused with Japanese flower arrangement which is an entirely different art and needs special training. A few flowers can just as effectively be arranged in a vase, especially if it is an urn, as being narrow at the top less flowers are required to make a satisfactory arrangement without it looking too empty. Bunches of flowers in a container with bun or reindeer moss is a very economical way to make a large arrangement from very few flowers. They can be arranged in baskets as already mentioned earlier or on a large dish.

Often the bun moss has quite a lot of soil on the back when it has either been gathered from the countryside or bought from the florists and some needs to be trimmed away to make it thinner and so easier to use. Moss once gathered will last a very long time, but while it is on the arrangement it has to be kept moist to keep it green so needs to be sprayed overhead with a mist spray. When it is not in use it can be left in the garden where the rain will keep it moist, but if there is a dry spell then it needs to be sprayed outside. In this way you can use it for many arrangements. If the moss seems insecure on the arrangement it can be pinned down on to the wire netting with pins made from bending hairpins or small pieces of stub wire in half. Reindeer moss will keep for a very long while, too. Even if this moss dries out it can be soaked again until it becomes spongy, and it can also be pinned into position. With an arrangement on a large dish the moss can be left in place for several weeks and the flowers changed when necessary, placing fresh ones in the spaces in the moss left by the now discarded flowers.

Many different flowers can be used such as grape hyacinths (*Muscari*), cyclamen, chincherinchee, *Dimorphotheca*, hyacinth, daffodils, daphne and a host of others. Branches are also attractive, either flowering ones or just bare branches to begin with in the winter which will gradually come into leaf and be an interesting indoor garden to watch. When making these gardens place the moss on the container first, leaving spaces for the flowers, and then if any netting is showing afterwards place small pieces of moss on to cover it. Pinholders can be placed under the netting to hold the taller flowers. The netting needs to be raised slightly higher in the container when using moss so that the moss does not touch the water. Any small pieces of trailing foliage such as ivy can be used as well as flowers to break the line of the container. The foliage will keep for several weeks.

One way of making a very few flowers look more impressive in a vase is to add branches of a shrub or tree; again it can be a flowering shrub or just a bare branch. Here are two arrangements which use only a few flowers and have branches and foliage with them. One uses three single rounded flowers which are chrysanthemum blooms, the other uses five gladioli, a pointed flower which can be difficult to arrange on its own.

The first arrangement is in a heavy pottery container of modern design. The shrub is *Viburnum fragrans*, the three

Twigs help to make flowers look more impressive. This heavy pottery container has three chrysanthemum blooms and twigs of Viburnum fragrans, *with three bergenia leaves to cover the wire netting.*

leaves are bergenia and the flowers three pinky red chrysanthemum blooms. The branches could be left in the container until the leaf stage and different flowers placed in with them from time to time. They would need to be quite large, bold flowers to balance the heavy pottery container. The bergenia leaves last quite a long time too. The container has wire netting in it and being deep it is unnecessary to use a pinholder. Establish the outline first with the viburnum. Place the first branch three-quarters of the way back in the container a little way in from the left side, as this arrangement is an off-centre facing. A piece of viburnum goes on either side of the longest one, each a different length. A fairly long branch is placed curved downwards on the right side and the one on the left is about half the length of the one on the right. Join up the main outline, decreasing the stem lengths as you go down from the tallest to the widest. Place in the chrysanthemum blooms so they are fairly centrally placed, one higher towards the back of the container a little to the right, one over the rim of the vase again to the right of centre and the largest flower to the left between these two flowers. Frame the flowers by placing in the bergenia leaves and as there is only a small opening in the container these should be sufficient to cover the wire netting. Place other pieces of viburnum through with the flowers.

The second arrangement is in a green pottery urn, which again has wire netting in it, but you could use florists' foam if you preferred. The pictures show the arrangement in three stages to illustrate how it is built up. Gladioli are often sent as gifts and this is one way that they can be arranged attractively. Being stiff upright flowers they do not always look comfortable being placed horizontally, which is why I placed them all relatively upright. Begin three-quarters of the way back in the centre of the container and place in the tallest flower then gradually make the rest of the flowers shorter as they come forward, keeping them quite close together. When this is completed as shown in the first picture you can then position the twigs. In this case, to pick up the colour of the yellow I have used the interesting flowers of *Hamamelis mollis* (witch hazel) which is so useful in the early spring. Instead of keeping the arrangement symmetrical, add a different emphasis by sweeping the *Hamamelis* from high on the left to low on the right. This accentuates the gladioli which can still be seen easily as in the second picture. Position pieces of *Hamamelis* through the centre. To give solidity to

To make a more interesting arrangement of five yellow gladioli in a green pottery urn, I placed them in the centre of the container, as shown in the first picture. The second picture shows Hamamelis mollis *sweeping from high on the left to low on the right. The completed arrangement in the third picture shows bergenia leaves placed in the centre with more* Hamamelis mollis *arranged through it and some azalea foliage coming from high on the right to low on the left. This arrangement is described in the text of this chapter.*

the arrangement and to make a focal point place three large bergenia leaves, one over the front, one slightly sideways and one at the back but facing towards the front. The mechanics need to be covered and, for this, autumn-coloured azalea foliage is used, picking up the

darker colour in the *Hamamelis* flower so that the colours are all linked in the completed arrangement.

A line arrangement is always effective with just a few flowers, and the arrangement of five arum lilies on a pinholder is quick to arrange as well as being unusual with their sculptured shape. The leaves of one particular flower should be used wherever possible. It would have been nice to use arum leaves in this arrangement, but because the leaves I had available were too large and would have overpowered the arrangement, I substituted the leaves of the scindapsus which are similar in shape but of a size more in keeping with the size of the container. The plate is of green glass, and as it is too shallow to put water into it, a large heavy pinholder is placed into a round metal container slightly larger than the pinholder. The arums are then arranged with the smallest at the top, gradually using larger and a little shorter flowers each

time as well as coming futher forward in the container. Keep a small flower for the one coming over the front of the container to the right of the centre. The shortest arum is the largest flower, to give depth to the arrangement. With arum lilies you can shape the stems so that they curve the way you wish them to by gently bringing your thumb down the side of the stem and curving the stem slightly at the same time. Arrange the leaves through the arrangement, keeping some well over the edge of the plate and making sure the pinholder and metal container are hidden, but keep part of the plate visible. As can be seen the leaves placed at the front are facing the leaves placed further back,

Above: Nine Euphorbia fulgens *in white with five bergenia leaves make this line arrangement in a large green pottery bowl which has a small container in it to hold the pinholder. The lovely arched sprays of this euphorbia can curve from side to side and the bergenia leaves are used around the base to give solidity and to cover the pinholder.*

Left: A line arrangement is a good idea when you only have a few flowers. This arrangement on a green glass plate containing a pinholder in a small dish uses five arums and leaves of the scindapsus.

and some are going sideways in the centre so that you can see the front of the leaf, adding interest to the arrangement.

These are only a few ways to use just a few flowers; similar flowers could be substituted in all these arrangements.

Flowers for the town dweller

Many people who live in town and do not have a garden have to rely on the florist for flowers and foliage for arrangements. Most florists have a wide range of flowers but it is usually more difficult to obtain interesting foliage, although with more

people taking an interest in flower arranging some florists do sell bunches of mixed foliage. Foliages such as eucalyptus and pittosporum are readily available and are extremely useful. The grey colouring of the eucalyptus is good with pink, blue or white flowers, and the eucalyptus which has coral-coloured buds is very attractive when used with flowers of the same colouring. The corkscrew-type eucalyptus has a fascinating shape, and only a few flowers need to be placed with it. Pittosporum with its fresh green colouring is lovely with yellow and white flowers.

To place with flowers bought from the florist, many interesting plant materials can be collected when visiting the country, and some will last for many weeks. It is surprising how many plants growing in hedgerows can be used in flower arrangements. There are many varieties of grasses, as well as hazel catkins in the spring; when the catkins are finished a branch of hazel can be used for a shape in line arrangements. A little later this will come into leaf. Alder trees, which grow near rivers and in damp places, have branches with small cones and catkins, and others to look out for are pussy willow, wild guelder rose, the leaves of wild arum, ivy – this may not be the variegated variety but it can still look pleasing especi-

ally with the seedheads of the tree ivy – small ferns and bracken, which can be used for foliage in the winter. Even bare twigs can achieve a pleasant arrangement.

Many arrangements can consist only of flowers and foliage from the florist. You could use 12 pink carnations with eucalyptus and carnation leaves, or 'grasses' as they are called. These could be arranged in an urn rather than a tazza, as an urn, being narrow at the top, does not need as many flowers as a tazza. With a facing arrangement in it and keeping it quite narrow in keeping with the shape of the container, the result looks quite elegant. The eucalyptus would last for several weeks and so when the carnations die the eucalyptus could be used again in

If you rely on a florist for flowers and foliage, you could use eucalyptus and iris as in this white pottery urn which has wire netting in it. The outline shape is achieved with the eucalyptus as in the first picture. The seven blue iris are placed fairly centrally through, having a small flower as the tallest one and gradually getting larger and shorter-stemmed flowers as one comes forward in the urn, saving a small flower to come over the front edge. Finish by placing more eucalyptus through with the flowers and short pieces to cover the netting until the arrangement is complete, as shown on the opposite page.

other arrangements. A line arrangement of blue iris on a dish or plate with the eucalyptus going through with the flowers is another idea.

If foliage is in short supply roses are a good idea, as you can use just the leaves from the roses. Where possible keep a small piece of stem with the rose leaves to help to hold the leaf into the netting or florists' foam.

Strelitzias will keep for some time and you need only three or five for a line arrangement or in an urn with some large leaves, either their own or from a pot plant, such as dracaena, *Begonia rex*, etc.

Mixed arrangements including daffodils when they are plentiful would make a change from using a limited number of flowers. These look well with pittosporum, and if you have been able to collect hazel catkins, these are an especially nice addition which gives that extra something to an arrangement.

The small spray carnations are economical to use as there are several flowers on a stem, and when arranging a smaller vase the side ones can be taken off and used separately. To have a slightly more unusually shaped container does help to add interest to an arrangement, especially when using one type of flower. The arrangement in the white dolphin container has eight stems of white spray carnations with small pieces of pot plant foliage. In Chapter 8 I mentioned growing various pot plants for use in flower arrangement and also flowers and foliage in window-boxes and on balconies. This does assist when foliage is difficult to obtain. The foliage I am using in this arrangement is ivy, peperomia and hebe. The container has a block of soaked florists' foam and over the top a small piece of wire netting, clipped over the edge of the container to hold it into position. The shape of the arrangement is an off-centre facing or asymmetrical. As the container has a shell on top of a dolphin this needs to be taken into consideration, as the shell is low and fairly flat. The flowers are arranged so that the longest flowers at the side spill out of the shell and the tallest flower at the top, which is a half-open bud, gives the illusion of the tail of the dolphin continuing upwards. The smaller flowers are kept around the edge of the arrangement and the larger ones nearer the centre. Keep the flowers a little closer to the container at the front edge, so as not to hide too much of the shell.

As with most facing arrangements, begin three-quarters of the way back for the main outline flowers, with the longest a little way in from the right edge. Place three flowers of varying lengths at the top, one on either side, the left one being longer than the right, and one over the edge at the front in line with the tallest one at the back. Take the secondary flowers from the stems and use these separately. The ivy foliage is placed high one side to low the other and the hebe goes the opposite way. The three peperomia are near the centre. Cover the netting with short-stemmed flowers and short pieces of foliage. Other flowers which could be used instead of the spray carnations are *Dimorphotheca*, anemones, small roses or small spray chrysanthemums.

An asymmetrical facing arrangement in a white pottery dolphin vase using eight stems of white spray carnations with hebe, ivy and peperomia foliage which could be grown in pots. This would be an economical arrangement as the spray carnations have several stems on them which can be used individually.

14 Arrangements for Special Occasions

Everyone likes to make a special effort with flowers for an important occasion. Here are some ideas as to the kinds of arrangements which would be appropriate for certain occasions. These will be mainly suitable for a home and some for a reception hall. Flowers for a church are described in the next chapter.

When arranging flowers for a particular event it is preferable, wherever possible, to arrange them the day before, so that on the day itself you can check to make sure they are all taking water properly and that all the flowers are keeping well. If any of them have drooped, these can be removed and others placed in. It is always worth while buying a few extra flowers for this purpose.

First I want to suggest which arrangements could be used for a family or friend's wedding. If the reception is to be held at home either in the house or a marquee then often the colouring of the bride's or bridesmaids' dresses or bouquets or a combination of both is used. This may not be easy if the furnishing in the house does not take the particular colour, as this also has to be taken into consideration. Linking the two if at all possible is a good idea, but if this fails then a neutral colouring of cream or white flowers would probably be the answer. If using the colouring of the bridesmaids' dresses it is easier when the colour being worn is yellow, apricot or yellow-pink; any of the blue shades or any colour which has blue in it can be inappropriate if the room is not very well lit, as blue does not show up well in poor light.

When the colouring has been decided the choice of arrangement comes next. A few large arrangements are more effective than many smaller ones. A large group of flowers where the bride and bridegroom greet their guests is very welcoming with another large group in the room where the reception takes place. If the room is exceptionally large, two or three groups would not look out of place. It is better to position these groups near the corners where they can be seen but not get in the way of the guests. If the reception is in a marquee, make sure that the pedestal on

which the flowers will be is stable, as often the ground is not very level. Preferably stake it to the ground, so that accidents do not occur.

The pedestal arrangement pictured is in white and lime green, and the flowers and foliage used are nine stems of lilac, 11 carnations, nine guelder roses (*Viburnum opulus*) used in their green stage, 11 iris, skimmia and rhododendron foliage, three stems of Longiflorum lilies and three bergenia leaves. As can be seen by the first picture three cones of different lengths are being used to obtain the required height. The pedestal is wrought-iron and the container is a mixing bowl, painted on the outside with matt black paint to match the pedestal. In the bowl is a large block of florists' foam which has been thoroughly soaked, over which is placed wire netting, tied into the container, as described in Chapter 7. Place the cones three-quarters of the way back in the container and in the centre, all close together with the tallest in the centre, as this is where the tallest flowers go in a symmetrical facing arrangement. Attach sticks to the cones before placing them into the container, as described in Chapter 4, page 31, and make sure they are firmly established in the foam and wire netting.

The main outline flowers are now placed into position. A lilac, which keeps better with its leaves removed from the stem, is placed in first in the tallest cone, with a guelder rose to the right of it and a lilac to its left, all placed in the same cone and each a different length. The widest flowers are placed in next with a lilac on the right and a guelder rose on the left. A guelder rose is the longest flower at the front and is in the centre. The grouping is lilac, carnations and skimmia going high on the left to low on the right and the guelder roses, iris and rhododendron foliage going the opposite way. Place in the three Longiflorum lilies next; these are the centre flowers. If the stem is not long enough the flower near the top can be placed in one of the cones. Choose the smallest flower for the lily highest in the arrangement, place another lily over the front edge on the left of the centre and a third, the largest one, near the centre but make sure that it is not in a straight line with the other two. The appropriate groups are linked through the arrangement, making sure a triangular shape is kept. Foliage needs to cover the front of the cones and go low over the netting so that the mechanics cannot be seen. Let the curved stems come well out over the rim of the container at the front. Any of the flowers that are not long enough to get sufficient height at the top can be placed in the cones. This arrangement would be suitable for a wedding reception and also for a church.

If small tables are being used at a wedding reception, a posy bowl, which is a small, low all-round arrangement, could be placed on each of them, remembering that their colours should be the same as for the main arrangements but with daintier flowers. If the tables are laid out in a formal manner, with a top table and sprigs coming from it, have two long, low table centres for the top table and one or two on each of the sprigs, depending on their length. The cake can be placed on a separate table and a cake top can be made with fresh flowers, again in keeping with the overall colour scheme, daintily arranged in a small silver vase or liqueur glass containing a small piece of florists' foam. Or you can do an arrangement of flowers placed in a small round of foam, covering the bottom half of it with kitchen foil. This can go straight onto the cake without having a container. If the cake is square the flowers can be arranged as a square to keep the shape of the cake.

If the reception is laid out as a buffet, then an arrangement on either side of the table, keeping the arrangements towards the back, looks attractive. These can be fairly high, preferably in containers with stems or stands, and not low as for a table centre. The arrangement in the silver meat cover is on a wrought-iron stand and is asymmetrical in shape. It is ideal for a buffet arrangement if two are arranged as a pair, with one on each side of the table so that the tallest flowers on each side are towards the outer edge of the table. The flowers used are sprays of philadelphus – which has had some leaves removed from around the flowers to prevent wilting, but not too many as it then detracts from the attractiveness of the spray – stripped lime, 11 roses, 11 carnations, alchemilla, periwinkle (*Vinca*), five peonies and five large variegated hosta leaves.

A piece of well-soaked florists' foam is placed to the left-hand side of the container – it would be to the right for the one going on the other side of the table –

Right: The main outline points of a pedestal arrangement in a mixing bowl which has been painted black and contains a block of florists' foam under wire netting. There are three cones which are placed three-quarters of the way back in the container and the flowers are grouped as for a facing arrangement.

Below: The pedestal arrangement completed for a wedding reception. It could also be used in a church or for any occasion where a large group is required. The flowers and foliage are grouped, with the lilac, carnations and skimmia foliage descending from high on the left to low on the right, and the guelder rose (Viburnum opulus), iris and rhododendron foliage going the opposite way. The centre flowers and leaves are three stems of Longiflorum lilies and three bergenia leaves.

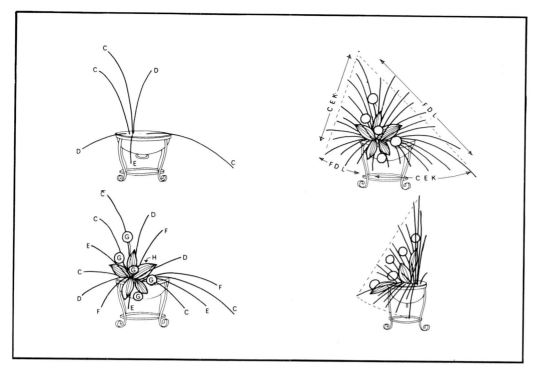

Left: Line drawings illustrating an arrangement which is suitable for a buffet table at a wedding reception. The container is a silver meat cover on a wrought-iron stand, and the flowers are in white and lime green. The main outline points are shown first, then, in the second diagram, the positioning of the flowers between the outline points together with the centre flowers and leaves. The overall shape is shown in the third picture and a side view of how it should look in the last. The flowers and foliage used are philadelphus (C), lime (D), roses (E), carnations (F), peonies (G) and hosta leaves (H).

the wire netting is then placed over the foam and secured to the wrought-iron stand in four places.

Begin the outline three-quarters of the way back in the container, a quarter of the way in from the left-hand side. Use a spray of philadelphus as the longest stem, curving slightly to the left. A second, shorter piece of philadelphus can then be placed to the left of this, curving in line with the first. These two stems should be close together to obtain a pointed shape at the top. A stem of stripped lime is placed to the other side of the tallest philadelphus, again close to it and curving away from the centre. To define the width on the right side, use a piece of philadelphus. This side is longer than the left and the stem should project well over the edge of the container with a downward curve. Also, because the meat cover is oval, the width of the finished arrangement should be slightly greater than the height. A piece of lime is used to mark the widest point on the left-hand side and this should be placed so that it too curves downwards. For the longest flower over the edge at the front, choose a small-flowered rose.

Use the peonies and hosta leaves to give weight and interest in the centre. Beginning with a small flower fairly near the top, zig-zag the peonies through the centre to one over the front edge to the right of the longest rose at the front. Place the largest peony in lowest near the centre. The hosta leaves form a frame for the flowers.

Fill in between the outline flowers; the groupings of the flowers in this arrangement are lime, carnations and periwinkle high on the right to low on the left and

the philadelphus, roses and alchemilla high on the left to low on the right. Place flowers and foliage throughout the arrangement, remembering the general principles. Check that the netting is covered and also that the arrangement looks correct from the sides.

As well as arrangements on the buffet table, garlands of flowers could be looped along the tablecloth. These are made on string. Flowers and foliage are wired with stub wires and then these stub wires are twisted around the string. The table holding the wedding cake could also have garlands around the cloth. In a marquee

A picture of the completed asymmetrical arrangement in the silver meat cover. A pair could be completed to go on either side of a buffet table.

An idea for a golden wedding is to arrange yellow flowers and foliage in the shape of a tree. A ball of florists' foam is placed at the top of a stick which can be covered with ribbon and the bottom of the stick is secured into a gold-painted flower pot with plasticine and pebbles or gravel. The flowers and foliage are inserted in the florists' foam as in the first picture and the completed arrangement looks like topiary work. A bow of ribbon can be placed at the base of the stick near the flower pot, as shown in the finished arrangement on the page opposite.

the poles could have garlands of flowers or just foliage twisted around them. Hanging baskets of flowers look pretty in a marquee, especially when a simple flower like marguerites are used with trailing foliage over the edge. These are also sensible to have because they are not in the way of the guests. You could also do arrangements on pieces of florists' foam which are in polythene bags with wire netting around them, as described in Chapter 7. These could be arranged in various shapes and hung from the poles in the marquee. If the reception was in a house, it might be convenient to have mantelpiece arrangements and also arrangements on windowsills, as they would be out of the way but still notice-able.

Another great celebration is a golden wedding, and one's thoughts immedi-ately turn to golden flowers. Very appro-priate they are of course on this occasion and look charming. But sometimes, if the furnishings are not in keeping with that particular colour, it is best to choose an alternative one such as the colour of the dress of the lady celebrating her golden wedding, or the furnishings of the house. Again, if it is a large party a ped-estal arrangement is a good idea, but if it is a smaller party, a group could look too formal so smaller arrangements placed around the house would be more pleasant.

If sending an arrangement as a gift for a golden wedding, a basket, sprayed with gold paint, or a brass vase or a bowl with gold and yellow flowers and foliage matching as much as possible, would be a very acceptable present. A spray or corsage placed on a parcel wrapped in

gold paper is a charming idea, and this could be worn afterwards. There is a dark cream orchid with a browner centre which would be very suitable for such an occasion, and preserved beech leaves could be placed around it. Another idea for a golden wedding is to place a round of soaked florists' foam onto a stick – this can be made of cane or be a stick from a tree – and put the other end of the stick into a flower pot which has a piece of plasticine in the bottom into which the stick can go. Then fill the pot up with gravel and tightly arrange flowers and leaves in the foam to resemble topiary work. The colouring could again be yellow or whatever the person's favourite colour is, or even mixed colours.

It is always very welcome to receive flowers on the birth of a baby. Small, dainty arrangements are nicer on these occasions. You can buy a container in the shape of a cradle. Place florists' foam into it and arrange a solid mass of flowers to look like a cradle cover, the flowers in the appropriate colour for the child. But probably the nicest arrangement is one in either pink or blue, or maybe both if it is a twin boy and girl, in a small basket or goblet. The shape could be facing or seen from both sides. A basket could also be sprayed with the appropriate colour. A christening arrangement could again be in pink or blue: if a christening party is to be held, then an arrangement on the buffet table would be ideal with a pedestal arrangement to match in the entrance hall.

For festive occasions such as Christmas or any party time you can be more adventurous with your arrangements using candles, artificial materials, and

fruit and vegetable groups – not forgetting the flowers! For parties as with any occasion it is attractive to have an arrangement in the hall to welcome your guests. Your choice will depend on the type of festive occasion, but try to keep the colouring appropriate for the celebration. For a cheese and wine party have a brightly coloured arrangement including grapes in it, black or green ones depending on the colour of the flowers being used. For a house-warming party red flowers are always fun, providing the furnishings of the house will not look wrong with them. Clashing red flowers are even better for this occasion and arranged in a copper container are fantastic. Different countries have different traditions for Christmas arrangements. In England a lot of evergreens is used, often large arrangements with just a few large red flowers. A ring of evergreens is usually placed on the front door. Evergreen garlands made in the same way as flower garlands for weddings look charming looped down the banisters, and these can look equally attractive made with dried or artificial materials, including ribbon. The dried material could be sprayed with paint in an appropriate colour for any country or for any festive occasion.

Often one large group is sufficient in a living room, having it in a distinctive colour or plant material. This could include fruit and vegetables with the flowers and foliage, in a festive colour, or using dried or artificial materials, you could incorporate a large bow of ribbon for the focal point. Decorated fir trees are popular for Christmas. It is nicer to decorate them using a colour scheme rather than having too many colours, and it also looks more effective. Colours which go well together are red, green and gold; silver, gold and green; blue and silver; red and gold, etc. An attractive way to decorate a tree is to use bunches of baubles in three's and five's, each having thin ribbon looped through the rings and each hanging at different levels. Attach them at the top with silver reel wire and a small bow of ribbon which is held in the centre by twisting silver wire round it. Then wire these bunches to the branches of the tree. Equally festive would be a bare branch sprayed with paint or left natural, whichever you prefer, and decorated with baubles in bunches, a lovely idea for any party in any country.

Wall plaques of artificial or dried materials placed into dry foam attached to a material-covered wooden base or polystyrene ceiling tile can be arranged in various shapes.

It is always pleasant to have flowers on a dinner table, and for festive occasions it

This facing arrangement would be good for a party. The first picture shows the main outline flowers, while the second has more flowers added around the periphery and three poinsettia and three bergenia positioned as the centre flowers and leaves. The picture opposite shows the completed *arrangement, with the group of five red roses, three orange gladioli, five stems of yellow spray chrysanthemums and escallonia foliage descending from high on the left to low on the right and three lilies, nine carnations and golden privet foliage going the opposite way.*

Opposite page: An arrangement suitable for Christmas. The container is a fondue-set base with a tray on it holding a pinholder in a small container. The beech twigs and tree ivy have been painted with glue and sprinkled with glass glitter. The twigs form the shape, through the centre of which are placed three red carnations and the tree ivy.

Right and below: Suitable for a festive occasion is this asymmetrical table centre. Once the candle holders have been fixed in the florists' foam and wire netting, the candles can be placed in position. Grapes and aubergines are attached to the netting with stub wires. The flowers used are two stems of white lilac, 11 spray carnations, five stems of white spray chrysanthemums and three cream gerbera with aubergine-coloured centres. The foliage is purple sage, Senecio greyii and santolina.

is lovely to have something special. Matching the colour to the table napkins, cloth or place mats is very effective. Candles are often included in these arrangements but if using them with any artificial materials keep them from burning too near to the pieces that could catch fire. Fruit with flowers are always appropriate in this room. A really clashing red including shocking pink is striking, using both flowers and fruit, as is a black and white arrangement which can look quite dramatic. An arrangement on a sideboard as a facing arrangement in a vase with a stem or stand to match the

one on the table can look very attractive. For a house-warming party arrangements in candle cups set into bottles are great fun. These arrangements usually include candles.

For a house-warming you can also have an arrangement in the kitchen. This is marvellous, using mainly fruit and vegetables with some foliage – you could always use the edible materials afterwards. The height of the arrangement can be achieved by using leaves such as sansevieria or any other exotic-looking ones. Pineapple with its lovely leaf top would look splendid as a focal point for

an arrangement using various coloured reds and oranges, such as dark red apples, oranges, carrots, red peppers and many others, with red-coloured foliage. As with flowers, try to get a variety of shapes with the fruit and vegetables. Of course if your kitchen is not suitable for orange or red colours you can choose other colour schemes. In a yellow and green range you could use a melon, avocado, bananas, green beans, green apples, pears, etc. Sometimes the fruit and vegetables will stay in place quite happily but if they do not, then place stub wires through the fruit or vegetable near the top, and wire

Right: Fruit and vegetables often need to be wired to hold them firmly into a container for flower arrangement, as described in this chapter. A selection have been wired here.

through either side of it, leaving four pieces of wire sticking out. Bend these to form a stem and twist them around each other to form a hook. This can then be hooked on to the wire netting in the position required. Alternatively cocktail sticks can be pushed up into the fruit or vegetable and these placed into the netting, but this is better for smaller fruits.

Finally, here are some unusual ideas for children's parties. One is to have pastel shades of flowers in a garden type of arrangement using bun moss over the wire netting in the container, and including twigs and bunches of pale pink, blue, green, yellow and mauve flowers. As well as the bunches of flowers, place in bunches of lollipops, in various colours.

Another very pretty arrangement is an all-round one in a low bowl, placing the flowers in very short in circles, rather as for a Victorian posy, and in the centre a fairly long stick covered with ribbon. From the top of the stick ribbons trail to each place at the table with a gift attached at the end. The effect is that of a maypole. You could arrange this using florists' foam. An arrangement for a side table could be a small branch placed into a pinholder in a metal dish on a flat platter with leaves at the base and attached to the bare branches small bags of sweets which the children could take home with them. I think that fairly simple arrangements usually work best and are nicest for children's parties.

Above and opposite page, bottom: An arrangement of fruit and flowers which would be especially suitable for the kitchen at a house-warming party. The picture on the page opposite shows the fruit and vegetables which are used. These are a pineapple, two leeks, five oranges, chillies, three carrots and three courgettes and they are placed in the container first, together with the outline flowers, orange gladioli and orange lilies. In the picture above the rest of the flowers and foliage have been added in an asymmetrical arrangement, but without obscuring the fruit and vegetables. The other flowers and foliage used are apricot chrysanthemum sprays and blooms and the leaves of monstera and croton.

15 Church Flowers

A small pedestal arrangement which would be suitable for Sunday services. It is a basic facing arrangement using 24 white carnations, pittosporum foliage and three bergenia leaves in the centre. The arrangement is in a green bowl which contains florists' foam with wire netting placed over it. A backing outline of pittosporum is established first as it is against a white background. The white carnations are then positioned throughout the arrangement.

Many people take great interest in arranging flowers in churches, whether for a church every week or for the many flower festivals for charitable organizations. The arrangements for flower festivals usually depict a certain aspect of the church or the area in which it is taking place; for instance, in country areas the arrangements often depict rural crafts. Sometimes the full colour range is employed by having darker flowers as one enters the church, going through to white flowers on the altar. These types of arrangements are very different from doing the flowers for the Sunday service, as often they have an accessory to help depict the theme and perhaps a drape if they are compositions. They can also pick up colours in stained glass windows and a swag or garland can be made to depict a carving, as done by Grinling Gibbons.

Before any flowers are arranged in church it is advisable to find out any 'do's' and 'don'ts' which a particular church may have. These might include where arrangements should be placed so as not to impede the progress of the choir, or in some churches it is not permissible to put flowers on the altar or in the chancel. Also it is best to find out if there are containers and pedestals or plinths already in the church which could be used. It is also worth finding out a suitable time to do the arrangements as it is rather frustrating to arrive with all your flowers and equipment only to find that there is a service in progress.

Make sure when arranging flowers in church that they are all stable and if necessary attach them to a pew or a rail, as they can easily be brushed against when many people are walking about, some in flowing surplices. Also be especially careful with the balance when arranging flowers in a church, or any large building for that matter: most of the congregation will be seeing them from a distance, so flowers need to be bolder and the arrangement quite large and solid. Do not try to compete with a high building by making the arrangement very tall and thin, as this tends to make one's eye look further upwards, so a large, solid, spreading arrangement with bold flowers and colours which show up well will arrest the eye and stop it travelling upwards.

First impressions are important when arranging flowers for a particular occasion in a church, so remember to arrange a good group at the entrance where it will be seen first and also last when the congregation is leaving the church. This can be in the porchway but as there is often insufficient room for a large pedestal arrangement, having it just inside the church is best. When arranging the flowers the church will be empty so you need to remember to have flowers above eye level, because those placed below will only be seen by the minority. This can be

achieved by pedestal arrangements, flowers on windowsills and fairly high ledges. Do make sure you do not place an arrangement where the vicar is going to be conducting the service.

Each week, churches usually have either one or two large groups beside the altar if flowers are not permitted on the altar or two altar vases if they are allowed, or perhaps one group and two altar vases. The groups can be arranged as described in Chapter 14, page 105. Altar vases are more difficult to arrange if they are the upright brass type. If this is the case and there is not sufficient room to put florists' foam into the neck of the container, then a candle cup or funnel could be attached to the top, as described in Chapter 4, page 30, and the flowers arranged in that. Sometimes there are mantel vases which are boat-shaped and have more space in which to arrange the flowers.

When arranging flowers each week in church, remember that if there is a particular church festival then the flowers should be in the appropriate colour.

An L-shaped arrangement on a windowsill which picks out the red colour from the stained-glass window. The arrangement is in a painted baking tin in which there is florists' foam with wire netting over it. The flowers used are five gladioli, seven roses, nine carnations and five alstroemeria. The foliage, pale green to lighten the red flowers, is erica, skimmia and hebe with three bergenia leaves. Gladioli, carnations, erica and skimmia make one group, alstromeria and hebe another, roses and bergenia a third.

Different shaped arrangements are suitable for different positions in churches. The facing arrangement is, of course, suitable for large or small arrangements. When doing arrangements as a pair, one can do symmetrical facing arrangements but the asymmetrical look is probably nicer as the longer of the two sides can go towards each other and the shorter sides can be placed against a pillar or wall. The off-centre facing and the L-shaped are both suitable. The off-centre is more useful as a pedestal arrangement. The L-shaped is excellent for such positions as the chancel steps, one being placed on one side, the other on the opposite side. It is better to keep the tallest side to the line of the wall. L-shaped are also very good on windowsills in pairs or singly especially if there is a stained glass window which you do not want to cover. The height of the arrangement should go against the outside edge of the window and the lower side under the window. Often an arrangement on just one side is better than having one on either side.

Asymmetrical arrangements can also be used on the altar, either the off-centre or the L-shaped. The longest side can go towards the cross. The L-shaped is better arranged in a trough-shaped container. The arrangements should be smaller than the cross so as not to look overpowering.

As has already been mentioned in an earlier chapter, blue flowers and those which contain a proportion of blue do not show up very well in dark places, and as churches are often fairly dark, try to avoid these colours and use ones which do show up well. If blue is being used with other coloured flowers, make sure that the blue flowers are not used on the periphery of the arrangement where they cannot be seen distinctly from a distance, as this will distort the shape of the arrangement.

Possibly the time I like best in decorating a church is at harvest festival, when a great variety of fruit and vegetables as well as flowers and foliage are brought to the church and there is great scope with the arrangements – windowsills with large arrangements of mixed coloured flowers, fruit and vegetables, or a few choice pedestal arrangements in autumnal colouring. As a child I can always remember the pillars of the church twined with wild clematis, simple but very pleasing. For a harvest festival the fruit and vegetables are better not wired as they are generally distributed to the sick and elderly afterwards, but care should be taken to place them in such a way that they are not likely to roll off.

When doing flowers in the church for a wedding as with doing the flowers for the wedding reception, the colouring can be linked with the colour of the bride's or bridesmaids' dresses. Personally I prefer it to be the bride's dress in the church as often she wears white or cream and these are very good colours for church as they show up so well. It is better anyway to have white or cream flowers on the altar, and something simple rather than too mixed – a few stems of lilies are often sufficient.

Three quite large groups of flowers are usually enough for a wedding, one at the side of the altar, one at the chancel steps on the opposite side to where the one at the altar is placed, and one at the entrance. The colours, if taken from the bridesmaids' dresses, could have white or cream included too. If the bridesmaids are wearing blue, just keep the blue colouring near the centre of the arrangement. Ideal colours for bridesmaids that show up well are yellow and salmon shades. Often pew ends are made for a wedding and are placed on the pews at equal intervals down the aisle. These are made as I have described in Chapter 7, page 48.

At a christening the main area of the church to decorate is around the font. If the vicar does not object, a wire frame is ideal with spagnum bound on to it, and bun moss pinned over this into which small containers are placed at equal distances around the frame, leaving a space where the vicar stands. In the containers place small dainty flowers of blue or pink, depending on whether the child is a boy or girl. If a frame is not allowed then a pedestal arrangement nearby or some flowers arranged around the base of the font look attractive. Flowers should also be placed on the altar.

Having a checklist as to what to take is helpful and you will find the following items very useful when doing church flowers: scissors, secateurs, wire netting, wire (both reel and stub), ready-soaked florists' foam, pinholders, string, cones or tubes, vases, dust sheets, pedestals, brush and brush pan, watering can and, if there is to be a large arrangement or an arrangement on a high windowsill, etc. and no steps are available at the church or one of its adjoining buildings, a step ladder.

Whenever possible, it is easiest to take the flowers in the car in buckets of water rather than having them placed in boxes too long without having a drink. Buckets placed between the front and back seats of a car stay quite firmly. This saves a lot of time taking the flowers from boxes and placing them into buckets.

A pew end in shades of yellow which is suitable for a wedding. How to make the base is described and illustrated in Chapter 7, page 48. The flowers are pushed through the polythene bag into the florists' foam, those at the bottom being longer than those at the top. The widest point of the arrangement is about a quarter of the way from the top, and the flowers need to be built out from the top and the bottom to the widest point. The flowers and foliage used are alstroemeria, border carnations, chrysanthemum sprays, roses, gerbera, privet and ivy foliage, with bergenia leaves for the centre.

16 Flowers for Room Settings

An arrangement in a brass jug which is suitable for a cottage home. It is completed as for a basic asymmetrical arrangement. The flowers used are orangy-yellow border carnations, skimmia and orange tulips. The foliage is honeysuckle and croton leaves.

When choosing what kind of flower arrangement to place in a room, you need to consider the colour scheme of the room and the style of furnishings, before deciding the colour and type of flowers, and also the container in which the flowers are to be arranged. On the whole, classical styles need classical arrangements, cottage homes need more garden-type flowers and modern rooms need the more unusual containers, but having said this you should not take this advice too literally as there are exceptions and it is fun to experiment with different kinds of arrangements in all rooms.

First the conventional ways of putting flowers in a room. The elegant country house needs large arrangements otherwise they would be too small to be noticed. The pedestal arrangement in a Georgian urn is impressive in this setting. A long, low arrangement is best on a cabinet over which is a painting, choosing the colouring for your flowers from the painting. For festive occasions mixed foliage arrangements are effective with mixed foliage garlands down the staircase looped through with ribbons. In the dining-room use a candelabra with candle cup arrangements in it, an epergne flowing over with flowers or a large centrepiece arranged in two or three layers which includes fruit with the flowers.

In the cottage-type home, with cosy log fire, basket arrangements always look at their best, some with daisy-like flowers such as marguerites or marigolds or mixed garden flowers. Arrangements in brass and copper look beautiful – the old copper jug with flowers in orange or red, having the flowers high on the side of the handle and the flowers coming longer and lower on the side of the lip of the jug, so as to look as if they are pouring out of the jug. Arrange flowers in china containers which have a coloured pattern on them, again picking out the colours for your arrangement. In summer, as has been done for centuries, large mixed foliage arrangements can be placed in the inglenook fireplace.

The classical town houses and fairly formal arrangements go together well: the facing arrangement in a tazza, an arrangement in an urn in a niche, a small bowl of flowers on the hall table. Low table centres are best in the dining-room, a long one on a rectangular table, an oval one on an oval table and an all-round bowl on a round table.

For modern-designed rooms cylinder containers are a good choice or heavy pottery ones. Brightly coloured containers, which could be in heavy plastic, can be most attractive with the right kind of flowers in them.

The colouring of arrangements needs to blend well with the furnishings and not look too obvious, but naturally you do not want the same colour scheme all the time or, for that matter, the same flowers. The flowers do alter to a certain extent with the seasons, and in many ways it is better to have seasonal flowers. When a room is designed around two colours you can emphasize one of these colours one week and the other the next week. The third week the two colours could be blended together. You need not use the exact colour but a tint or shade of the colour. This will again give interest. You can also vary the containers, so that the shape of the arrangement will change, too. Use mixed flowers of the chosen colour or just one kind of flower, and change the position of the arrangement in the room. If a room has been furnished in neutral colours then an arrangement in brighter colours will be attractive. A Dutch group could be used in this case. If there is a painting on the wall, compose an arrangement using flowers in the same colours. A mirror is a useful feature because by creating an arrangement of mixed greens to reflect into it an impression of coolness can be achieved, which is especially effective in hot weather. Use an L-shaped arrangement of green to half-frame the mirror.

When sending a gift of flowers, try to remember the colouring of the room they will be going in. If this is not known, keep to neutral colours like cream. It is important to take into account the light intensity of the room. As I have already mentioned, blue is a very poor colour if

Three stages of an arrangement in pinks in a silver meat cover which would be suitable for a fairly formal room. It is completed as a basic facing arrangement. The flowers used are five gladioli, seven stems of chrysanthemum spray, 14 pink carnations and three alstroemeria. The foliage consists of three bergenia, ivy and eucalyptus. The first picture shows the outline flowers. In the second more outline flowers have been added and some of the foliage has been positioned. The completed arrangement is shown above.

the room is fairly dark, or any colour which has blue in it such as the blue-pinks, blue-reds and purples. Any blue flowers should be intermingled with brighter ones and never used on the periphery of an arrangement. Keep blue for daylight rather than artificial light. Yellow colours and colours with yellow in them will always show up well.

You can sometimes successfully blend antique furniture with modern containers and vice versa. An antique oil lamp which has been converted into a container can look well in a modern room. The bamboo cylinder container, partly because it is bamboo, can look quite good with antique furniture. In it are three stems of Singapore orchids and five bergenia leaves. As the flowers are quite simply arranged they would not detract from the furniture. The bamboo vase is fitted with an inner container to prevent the bamboo from coming into contact with water, which would cause it to split. The lining is made from a plastic washing-up liquid container, and has wire netting in it.

The three orchids are placed in first, the tallest three-quarters of the way back in the centre with the top curving gently away from the centre. The second shorter-stemmed orchid is placed to the right side of the first and a little further forward in the netting. The third stem, shorter and more forward still, is positioned to the other side of the tallest flower. Flowers removed from the bottom of the orchid stems can be used in helping to cover the wire netting so that it is concealed from view.

Above: A small white china basket filled with blue and white flowers which would be suitable for a bedside table. A description of how it is arranged is given in this chapter.

Left: A simple arrangement in a bamboo cylinder with three spider or Singapore orchids and bergenia leaves. The shape needs to be slender. This arrangement would look attractive in a room containing antique furniture.

The five leaves are placed around the base of the flowers to cover the netting and to add weight. The tallest goes at the centre back, a leaf on either side near the front, with the other two leaves going under the rest of the leaves to cover the netting.

Usually flowers in a guest bedroom are kept to small arrangements, perhaps a small arrangement of roses on a bedside table or dressing table, or even a single flower in a vase. The arrangement in the small white china basket needs to have dainty flowers in it and it is also pleasant to include some flowers which have a strong perfume – in this basket the freesia, small pieces of philadelphus and pinks. The flowers are in blue and white and are small side branches of philadelphus – some in flower and others as seedheads – white freesia, blue alpine campanulas, a few white pinks and dark blue cornflowers. The foliage is rue, small trails of ivy and three small hosta leaves.

As the basket has a handle, part of it should be seen in the completed arrangement. A piece of florists' foam is placed in the container. A seedhead of philadelphus establishes the tallest point to the left of the handle, the second flower is a bud of a pink and is on the right of the handle and is a little shorter than the tallest flower, and the third flower at the top to the left of the first flower is philadelphus. All are placed three-quarters of the way back in the container. To make the width a philadelphus flower is positioned on the right and a freesia on the left. The width is wider than the height as the container is fairly low and wide. The longest flower at the front is a philadelphus. When the main outline is completed, place the dark blue cornflowers near the centre with the hosta leaves. Then connect the outline flowers and foliage and the flowers and foliage through the centre. Group the freesia, pinks, campanulas and rue from high on the right to low on the left and the flowers and seedheads of the philadelphus and the ivy the opposite way, as there are quite a large number of sprigs of philadelphus. Check the netting is covered.

As has been suggested earlier, for a party a kitchen arrangement is fun to have but it is also pleasant to have flower arrangements in the kitchen at any time, often including fruit and vegetables. These look particularly attractive in a pine kitchen.

17 Dried Flowers

Dried flowers can be very useful when flowers are expensive or in short supply in the garden in winter-time. I do feel though that when you put a dried arrangement in a room there is a tendency to leave it there the whole winter, by which time I am sure everyone is thoroughly tired of it, as well as it being full of dust! In theory it would be good to change it once a week as you would fresh flowers, not necessarily using completely different dried material, but at least using another container and adding other colouring, but I am afraid this never works with me.

Having a dried foliage base for an arrangement is quite useful and a few fresh flowers can be added each week to provide interest.

There are many kinds of dried and preserved flowers and foliage on the market these days which are quite easily obtainable. Unless you have plenty of surplus space in the garden, it might be better to buy them as the cost of buying fresh flowers and foliage as well as preserving materials would not be really worthwhile. However, if you do have room to grow suitable subjects and have suitable plants in the garden or access to plant material which dries well, then of course it is worth preserving them.

The easiest method of preserving plant material is air-drying. Flowers need to be cut just before they are fully open – if they are too old they are liable to shatter, if too young they may wilt. Remove all the leaves from the stems. If the flowers are particularly fragile you can drop some clear glue from a cocktail stick at the base of the petals to hold them together. Tie the flowers together in small bunches and hang upside down in an airy room which is free from damp. Suitable flowers for this method include *Helichrysum* (straw flower), ornamental grasses, statice, honesty (*Lunaria*), both red and green varieties of love lies bleeding (*Amaranthus*) – be careful the tails do not get tangled – Chinese lanterns (*Physalis*), *Astilbes*, achillea, globe thistle (*Echinops*), bells of Ireland (*Mollucella laevis*) and delphiniums.

Flowers can be dried in a strong cardboard box, using two parts borax and one part silver sand. They should not touch each other and should be completely covered. If you put a piece of cardboard under each flower the mixture can be more easily distributed around the flowers. Take care not to squash the flowers. Flowers can also be dried in silica gel in a polythene bag. The flowers go on a layer of silica gel in the bag and then the bag is carefully filled with it ensuring that it gets between all the petals of the flowers. Take care not to let the flowers touch each other. Seal the bag and hang it up in a fairly warm place for about one week, but this does vary depending on the flowers; it could be less or

An arrangement of dried material in a dark green tazza with a tall stem which has dried florists' foam fixed into it with wire netting. The height is established with the grasses, and the glycerined eucalyptus is swept from high on the left to low on the right. The hydrangea and lotus heads are placed near the centre.

slightly more. When the flowers are dried, gently remove all the silica gel and store the flowers in a bag in which a few of the crystals have been placed. Examples of flowers dried in either borax and sand or silica gel include zinnias, gerbera, hellebore, achillea, roses, dahlias and many more – it is always worth trying for yourself to see if a certain flower does dry well or not.

Another very simple way of drying is by preserving leaves underneath a carpet or rug. Carpets are ideal but unfortunately with fitted carpets this is not always possible. It is almost worth having one room which does not have a fitted carpet. First, put down newspaper, carefully place on the leaves and then put newspaper over the top of the leaves, replacing the carpet or rug. By walking over it the leaves become pressed. If you prefer, you can place newspaper onto cardboard, then a layer of leaves on top of this, then newspaper; after making several layers like this finally place cardboard on the top and weight this down with something very heavy. Leaves which press successfully include leaves of maple (*Acer*), sumach (but these need to be gathered before they are too old), all kinds of ferns and brackens and small branches of trees.

Some flowers and leaves will dry by placing their stems in water and letting them dry gradually. Examples include hydrangea, viburnum, elaeagnus and eucalyptus. Hydrangea need to be picked at the right stage, when the petals are beginning to become firm. The green hydrangea will stay green if kept away from sunlight but will go brown if in sunlight, though this can be a very attractive colour.

Some leaves and indeed a few flowers can be preserved in a solution of glycerine and water. First hammer the bottom of the stems or split them for about 50 mm (2 inches), then place them in a sol-

A brown ovenware dish containing dried florists' foam with wire netting over it is here used for a basic L-shaped arrangement. The picture on the left shows the main outline, with the wood roses placed near the centre. On the right is the completed arrangement in browns, yellows and oranges and including various ornamental grasses, Helichrysum, Chinese lanterns, fir cones and glycerined box.

ution of one part glycerine and two parts hot water in a narrow upright container. Leave for about one week to ten days or until they change colour – many turn brown. Do not leave too long as the beads of moisture then tend to come out through the leaves. Beech leaves can be preserved in this way. If they are cut earlier in the year when they are firm, they will stay a greener colour; if they are cut later but before the sap has gone from the stems, they turn a golden brown. Do not leave it too late or all the leaves will drop off. Other materials which can be glycerined are eucalyptus, forsythia, oak, mollucella flower, hydrangea and

stripped lime. To prepare stripped lime, remove the leaves, leaving the bracts and flowers. These need to be glycerined just before the buds of the flowers open; if they are open they tend to look untidy when glycerined. These are particularly attractive branches for winter use. The foliage of berberis turns bright red if glycerined in the spring and brown when it is gathered in the autumn.

If stems need to be kept straight when drying and preserving them, or need to be strengthened, then a wire can be placed up into the stem. For hollow-stemmed flowers such as zinnias it is advisable to use stub wire with a hook

Honesty, grasses, hydrangea and pressed bracken, together with three gourds, are positioned on a round wooden tray for this dried arrangement. The grasses are kept at the top, with the honesty grouped one way and bracken the opposite. The gourds and hydrangea are placed near the centre and all the stems are held in position by dried florists' foam.

made at one end. Push the other end of the wire through the face of the flower and down inside the stem until the hook is firmly into the face of the flower.

Arrangements using dried materials are completed as for fresh flower arrangements, but if no fresh flowers are being placed into the arrangement, they can be arranged in dry florists' foam. If a few fresh flowers are going to be arranged with the dried material and the dried material is going to be in water then it is advisable to varnish the bottom part of the preserved stem which will help to prevent it from rotting and so disintegrating. Alternatively the fresh flowers

could be placed in cones in the dried arrangement and water just placed in the cones. These would need to be hidden by the plant material.

Dried flowers can also be arranged as a picture using a frame with a material-covered ground. Dry florists' foam can be attached to the ground and an arrangement placed into it. Dried materials can also be made into a garland or collage; much shorter stems are needed for this. Some flower material can look a little flat so extra care in the placement is required. To add interest try to have branches going a little sideways, so as not to see the leaves facing the front.